TABLE OF CONTENTS

Introduction: Why an online presence is critical in today's world..............1

Part I: Web design: The subliminal signals that win trust..........................8

1. The purpose of your website..10
2. Website buying environments: Set the tone for a sale..........................22
3. How many pages? What pages?...35
4. Structure of an inner page...42
5. How to write your About page..48
Your Edge Design...55

Part II: Copywriting: Hypnotize your website visitors............................60
6. Start with YOU..62
7. Know your USP..65
8. Humanize your business...73
9. Think like a designer Secrets of the written word.............................79
10. Transformations, identity and selling the result...............................89
Your Edge Copywriting...94

Part III: Marketing: The myth of instant inbound leads..........................100
11. SEO: The #1 strategy to rank in Google's top 5 search results.........102
12. Blogging: The secret to blogging success....................................108
13. A book: How becoming an author can grow your business...............116
14 Advertising: The most important principle to win sales...................124
15. Social Media: 3 strategies to reel in leads...................................129
Your Edge Marketing...135

Conclusion: The future of online business...140

Introduction

Why an online presence is critical in today's world

It's an ordinary day at your office. The sun shines, the birds chirp and you hear the gentle tap of fingers on keyboards. But something's off.

Everything feels a bit emptier.

You go outside for a breath of fresh air. While once upon a time, you'd see people shopping, twentysomethings lounging at cafes and customers walking in your door, now your neighborhood seems like a ghost town.

The sidewalks are empty, storefront lights are dark and the breeze feels chilly. Where is everyone?

They're online.

They're checking out Amazon's latest sale. They're sipping lattes with friends over Zoom and chatting about trendy new products they've found online.

How did this happen?

The world's digital transformation has accelerated

There's no denying the last 10 years have seen drastic changes in how people live.

Malls continue their trot to extinction. Ecommerce retailers like Amazon, Walmart and Alibaba are among the world's wealthiest companies. And video meetings are now unavoidable.

No matter how you feel about the Covid pandemic, one thing is certain—the digital transformation has sped up. In fact, according to leading ecommerce research company Digital Commerce 360, online sales increased 32.4% (nearly 200 billion dollars) from 2019 to 2020, two years faster than projected.

If you're not generating business from your online efforts now, you may feel left behind. You may fear your business won't survive.

But it's not too late.

There are still huge, life-changing opportunities for business owners, solopreneurs and freelancers. As Jeff Bezos has said, when it comes to the internet, "It's still Day 1."

How this book can help you succeed online

Whether you're new to online business or own a website that converts a few sales monthly, the potential for profits is huge. In fact, you could almost say it's infinite.

There are no boundaries online.

A brick and mortar store that only serves local customers is limited by the number of people in that neighborhood and the store's staff capacity. An online business, however, can sell to people from around the world and doesn't need one salesperson per customer.

You probably have many questions.

"How do I create an attractive website? How do I ensure people can find it? How do I persuade website visitors to buy from me?"

When you're just starting, all these questions can overwhelm you. There's so much to learn, do and you still have a business to run, or a full-time job. You may feel lost.

No need to worry.

This book is your shortcut. The goal is to build a foundation for your online presence, and then gain momentum as you optimize your website to attract sales and leads.

Over the past six years, I've helped hundreds of clients refine their website design, write irresistible copy and market their businesses. On the side, I've also sold over $100K worth of digital products. And that number continues to grow.

Now I want to show you a faster path. One that I've learned through experiences with my clients, years working at marketing agencies and my own online ventures.

But first, it's important to be aware of a common pitfall. And that starts with asking yourself two important questions...

Does your website work for you? Or do you work for it?

The truth is, most websites are useless. According to Ahrefs, a leading keyword research tool, 90.63% of web pages get 0 traffic. To put that in context, billions of websites go months and even years without anyone seeing them.

So instead of traffic and sales, business owners get nothing but a yearly bill. Their websites are jobless. Like unemployed digital citizens who collect a welfare check. Except that check isn't coming from the government—it's coming from you. What is a jobless website?

Basically, it's purposeless. Jobless websites aren't optimized for a specific goal: to sell your product, services or brand. And this is why many websites fail. Because each page, image, sentence and design element aren't aimed at the same goal. More on that later.

What you'll learn

This book's goal is to build a solid foundation for your online presence, which encapsulates three critical digital marketing skills: web design, copywriting, marketing. For your website to succeed, each of these components must work well. Why?

Because if your marketing and copywriting are great but your website's design is terrible, you won't capture leads.

If your copywriting and web design rock but your marketing sucks, you won't get traffic.

And if your marketing and web design are stellar but your copywriting is dull, you'll get thousands of people visiting your website only to bounce away after a few sentences.

If this sounds like a game of whack-a-mole, don't worry. It will become less overwhelming in the chapters ahead. And speaking of which, this book is divided into three parts—each focusing on the aforementioned skills. You'll learn about the ideal website page count, website buying environments, the #1 SEO tactic, how to use a book to promote your business and much more.

Note, however, this book is not the be-all and end-all on these topics and I won't get into the technical side of web design or marketing. Instead, you'll learn principles and strategies to transform your website into your most successful salesperson, and marketing techniques that ensure a constant stream of prospects come through your digital doors.

This book will teach you how to get started and increase leads, traffic and sales. Will the journey be easy?

Of course, not. And anyone who tells you otherwise is lying.

It took me five years to successfully make my business 100% online, where I now passively generate thousands of dollars in monthly sales and have the freedom to live around the world. Could you do the same in less than a year? Absolutely. Could it take you more than five? Yes, it could be much longer.

My point is, succeeding online is a challenge and the journey will differ for each person. But it's a worthwhile challenge. Like any new skill, it can be learned and you'll improve if you persevere.

If you're a beginner, you may feel nervous. You may want to procrastinate. But the key is to jump in. You will fail. Keep going. Try again and you'll slowly gain momentum.

I've also included my top three strategies for how to excel in the "Your Edge" chapters at the end of each of this book's three parts. Some of the strategies are concrete tactics, while others are principles to guide you. All of them will help you further accelerate your results.

Whether you're a newbie or have owned a website for years, you'll learn how to cut through the noise on the web as you reinvent your business online.

Part I

Web design: The subliminal signals that win trust

Trustworthiness probably isn't a characteristic most people request in their website's design. Instead, they want it to look modern, sleek and include parallax effects.

But if you want your website to attract new customers, appearing trustworthy is critical. How is trust communicated? Modernness, sleekness and parallax effects can all do the job—showing your website and business are up-to-date and not stuck in the '90s.

But there are other ways to reveal credibility. And that's what Part I of this book is about.

From website buying environments, to the purpose of your website, inner page structure and more, each element discussed in the following pages focuses on winning your visitors' trust. As you'll soon learn, how you communicate credibility will vary depending on your product and your business. And this section will give you an idea of your options.

There is, however, one thing all high-converting websites have in common. And that's the subject of this first chapter.

1.

The purpose of your website

This book's Intro discussed how every website needs a job. Without one, it does nothing but send you a monthly bill. Because purpose is critical to your website's success, this entire chapter is dedicated to the topic.

So let me drop a website bombshell on you.

Your website is not about you or your business

Seriously. It's not.

Most business owners love to gush about their product, service or brand. Their intentions are good. They likely believe that spreading their company's message is in everyone's best interest.

The reality is, few people will buy your product, like your social media pages or become rabid fans because you proclaim its awesomeness. Why?

Well, because people are self-centered. Now don't take this personally. Hear me out. Imagine you're having a conversation at a party and one guest starts going on about his business, as if he's boasting about his firstborn child, will you listen to him intently for 10 minutes? I doubt it. You'll likely tune out or excuse yourself to the bathroom or to refill your beer.

This happens because the proud business owner was focused on himself—not his audience. There's nothing to be ashamed of if you do this. It's human nature to put yourself and your needs first. Which is why you need to change your perspective and take advantage of this natural tendency.

The marketing paradox shift—from **me** to **you**

Every section of this book—web design, copywriting and marketing—are part of the same thing: marketing. Your website's purpose is to market your business as is your copywriting. And marketing, well, is of course marketing.

Anyone who's found some success in these will know the simple truth I'm about to share. Marketing is all about the customer, fan, lead or even the party guest listening to you. It's not about you or your business, it's about what your business does for them.

When you understand this, your focus shifts from talking about how great your business is, to talking about what your business can do for customers. Instead of looking at the customer through the eyes of your business, you look at your business through the eyes of your customers.

Your site must fulfill the needs of your customer. If it doesn't, then they will bounce.

Why your website needs to be a sexy tease

Teases usually aren't desirable. Who would pick a tease over the full monty?

When I worked as a television writer a decade ago, I learned just how important a good tease is. Without one before the commercial break, you lose viewers. The tease creates curiosity. And sparks one of the most important questions on the minds of anyone who reads, watches or listens to a story: "What's gonna happen next?"

The tease is the carrot on the string that keeps people coming back for more. And that logic applies to your website too. Your website should be the carrot that triggers them to pick up the phone and call you, send you a message or subscribe.

Many business owners fail at the website tease. Instead, they build a massive site with countless pages, cataloging dozens of products and services and the company's life story—overloading visitors with TMI. These business owners want to tell the visitor every last detail. And then what happens?

The visitor becomes bored, confused or lost in your content. So they leave.

Don't be like these websites.

Remember, your website is not about you or your business. It's really about the visitor. And the visitor wants to solve their problem.

Everyone's time is limited, especially the people visiting your website. They want to find the information they need quickly. When you drown them in content, you make their life difficult and maybe even give them a headache. You'd probably leave a website like this too.

This is why your website's purpose is critical.

The one purpose every website has in common

Whether your website represents your non-profit, small business, corporate empire or is even an ecommerce site, there is one purpose they have in common. All websites are designed to promote your brand.

Now don't get confused here. By "promote," again, I don't mean to gush about your business. Instead, I mean to **help the website visitor**.

If you're a non-profit like a summer camp, your service helps the website visitor with their children and, ultimately, visitors feel good about themselves for supporting your organization.

If you're an ecommerce website or small business that sells car parts, your website helps the customer buy a product that will improve their life, perhaps for a lower price than anywhere else.

If you're a big company like a bank, maybe you offer an online portal for customers to check their balances, open credit cards or transfer money. Again, you are helping the customer (in this case through convenience), which indirectly promotes your brand and increases customer loyalty.

As you move forward in this book and with your business, remember the following principle because it is infused in every aspect of digital marketing—focus on the customer, help the customer.

For websites, one purpose comes in many forms

Take a quick poke around online, and you'll soon see that not all websites look the same. They come in different forms and have different purposes.

But wait a second.

Didn't I just say all websites have one purpose?

I did, but that same purpose can be achieved in multiple ways and forms. Let's look at four popular examples.

The lead generation website

Many websites will fall into this category. A lead gen website's purpose is, well, obviously to generate leads. This is done by including a call to action or CTA (more on this later) that asks the reader to contact them, get a quote, subscribe to a newsletter, etc. My website ordinarydudemeditation.com is a good example of a lead gen website as its primary purpose is to capture email addresses. Here's a screenshot of what I mean below:

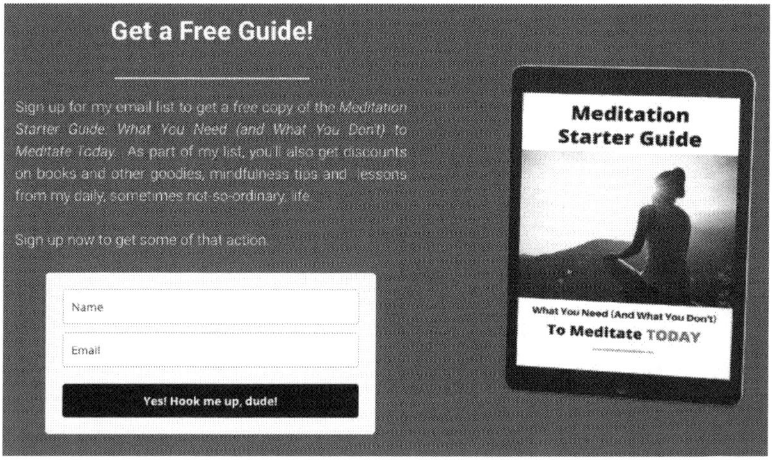

For a second example, check out SEO guru Neil Patel's website: https://neilpatel.com/

The ecommerce website

Another common type of website is an ecommerce site. For those unfamiliar with the term "ecommerce," it basically means to sell stuff online. The main purpose of these sites is to get customers to punch in their credit card details, which means products are front and center. To do that well, the ecommerce sites must clearly communicate, through design and copywriting, how each product helps visitors.

Even if you've never heard of ecommerce before, you're probably well aware of the world's largest ecommerce company: Amazon. To see an example of ecommerce in action, head over to Amazon or check out this mock book sales page for ordinarydudemeditation.com:

The blog

A blog promotes a business indirectly and helps visitors by sharing valuable advice and tips. When a website's main purpose is increasing blog readership, articles will dominate the homepage.

Now, this isn't to say other types of websites can't have a blog—many do. The difference is that a blog's core focus is to feature articles, which provide visitors helpful information usually related to the product. This wins visitors' trust and indirectly earns sales, leads and promotes the brand. Here's an example of a blog site from Ordinary Dude Meditation when it used to be a blog in 2020 and 2021:

Alternatively, Jon Morrow's excellent www.smartblogger.com offers another example.

The business card website

This type of website is short and sweet, usually a single page. It's more straightforward than your average website, as its goal is to quickly and clearly explain the business's offer and provide contact details. This type of site is great for freelancers. But for everyone else, I typically recommend a different style as the business card site doesn't generate immediate leads or sales. I've taken the liberty of designing a mock business card website for the purpose of this book (based on an older version of my own freelance site). You can check it out on the next page.

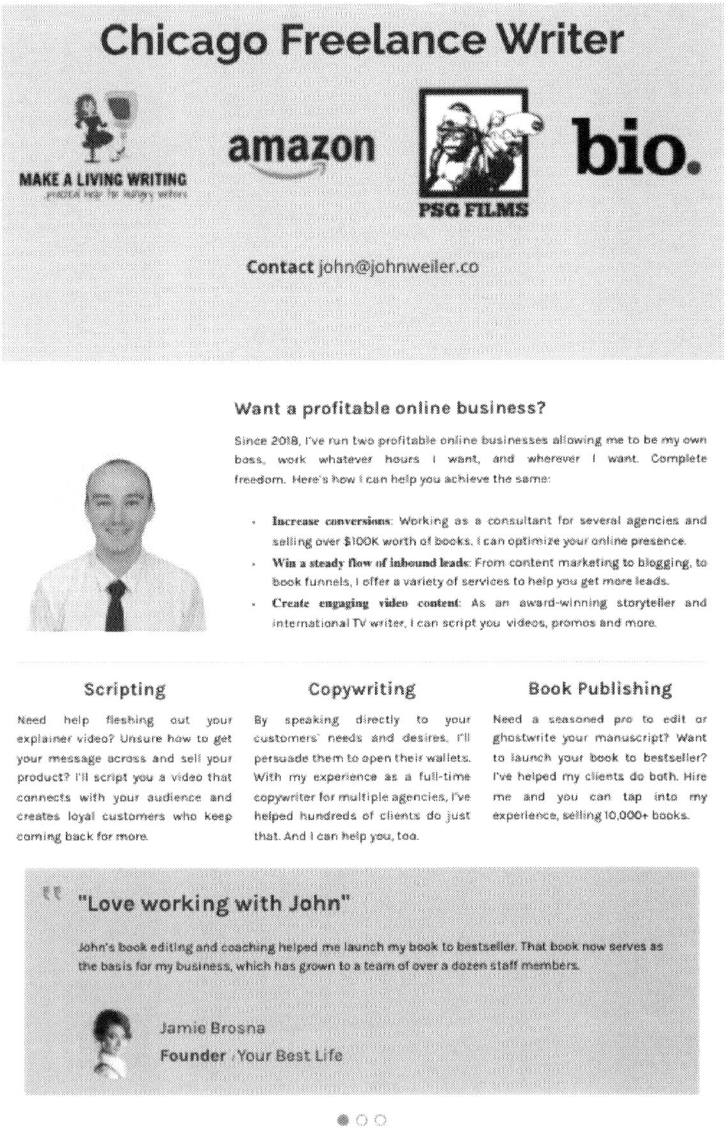

Chicago Freelance Writer

MAKE A LIVING WRITING

amazon

PSG FILMS

bio.

Contact john@johnweiler.co

Want a profitable online business?

Since 2018, I've run two profitable online businesses allowing me to be my own boss, work whatever hours I want, and wherever I want. Complete freedom. Here's how I can help you achieve the same:

- **Increase conversions**: Working as a consultant for several agencies and selling over $100K worth of books, I can optimize your online presence.
- **Win a steady flow of inbound leads**: From content marketing to blogging, to book funnels, I offer a variety of services to help you get more leads.
- **Create engaging video content**: As an award-winning storyteller and international TV writer, I can script you videos, promos and more.

Scripting

Need help fleshing out your explainer video? Unsure how to get your message across and sell your product? I'll script you a video that connects with your audience and creates loyal customers who keep coming back for more.

Copywriting

By speaking directly to your customers' needs and desires, I'll persuade them to open their wallets. With my experience as a full-time copywriter for multiple agencies, I've helped hundreds of clients do just that. And I can help you, too.

Book Publishing

Need a seasoned pro to edit or ghostwrite your manuscript? Want to launch your book to bestseller? I've helped my clients do both. Hire me and you can tap into my experience, selling 10,000+ books.

"Love working with John"

John's book editing and coaching helped me launch my book to bestseller. That book now serves as the basis for my business, which has grown to a team of over a dozen staff members.

Jamie Brosna

Founder / Your Best Life

And here's the link to the mock site: https://www.johnweiler.co/businesscard.html

Before moving on, note this list is not comprehensive and websites often fit into more than one category. For example, a blog could also be an ecommerce website, selling dozens of products nestled within its articles. A business card website could also generate leads. So my recommendation is to use the above as examples to consider when planning your website design.

2.

Website buying environments: Set the tone for a sale

In Joe Sugarman's book *The Adweek Copywriting Handbook*, he describes a concept called the buying environment. Every store and website has one, and it's critical to closing sales. What is a buying environment? Here's a simple definition:

A buying environment is the tone, feel or atmosphere of a store that puts the customer in the mood to buy.

Think of the buying environment like your shoppers' experience as they enter your store. To illustrate this concept, let me give you two examples of polar opposite buying environments.

The buying environment of Starbucks vs Goodwill

When you think of Starbucks and Goodwill, you probably couldn't imagine two different stores. One is upscale and smells delicious, the other is cluttered and smells like old clothes.

Each, however, has a buying environment.

Call me a yuppy, but I am a shameless Starbucks fan. They have a brilliant buying environment. From the wooden decor, dim but classy lighting, elegant music and delicious aroma of gourmet arabica beans, this place primes you to splurge on coffee. Starbucks isn't just selling you a cup of coffee. They're selling an experience that you smell, see and hear the second you step inside.

Goodwill also has a buying environment, it's just drastically different from Starbucks. Yes, it may look a bit cluttered and smell musty, but this is what prepares shoppers to buy. They see all the clothes, trinkets, books and other second-hand goods scattered about and think, "What sort of discounts and treasures will I find today?" This atmosphere excites customers, putting them in a buying mood.

What happens if you create the wrong buying environment?

Imagine if the interior of Starbucks was designed like McDonald's. Instead of classy music, a chic interior and gourmet baked goods on display, you see plastic booths, bright lights and dozens of workers behind the counter, working in what looks like a fast food factory. Would you spend $5 for a cup of coffee?

Probably not. The buying environment doesn't provide the upscale experience customers expect.

The same thing goes for Goodwill. Imagine if a customer walks in, expecting to find deals and goodies, but encounters an interior decked out like Louis Vuitton—an organized, classy, uncluttered space with sales reps in expensive outfits, strutting about on posh marble flooring. I bet you that Goodwill shopper runs in the opposite direction. There's no way he'll find a great discount in such an upscale store.

The buying environment must match your buyers' expectations and prepare them to buy a product priced in line with the experience.

Your website must also set the tone for action, just like a brick and mortar store

Yes, it's true. Websites also have buying environments. However, while a store creates an experience that affects all senses—sight, sound, smell, touch, taste—a website's buying environment is typically only visual. That said, those visuals can still prepare your visitor to take action.

Website buying environments

Just as we did with Starbucks and Goodwill, let's look at two very different online buying environments: Trader Joe's and Apple computers.

Let's start with Apple.

But first, a quick note. To show screen grabs of Apple's website would require permission from the Steve Jobs' empire, which would be a long, tedious process. I don't have time for that. So instead, I've created a similar site—this way you'll get the gist of online buying environments without having to leave this book. I live in Thailand, so let's name the similar site after my favorite Thai fruit: Mango.

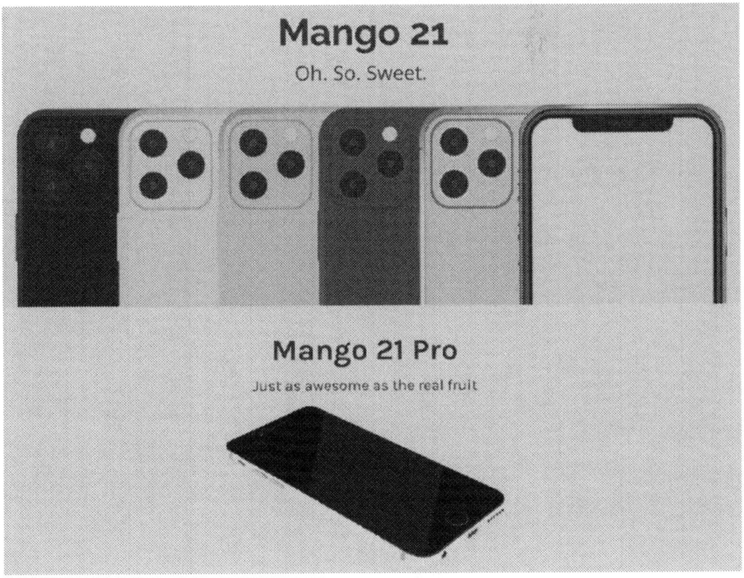

Mango Watch

Wear it every day. Keep the doctor away.

Mango TV

As irresistible as a big, beautiful mango

Mango Seeds

Let music grow your inspiration

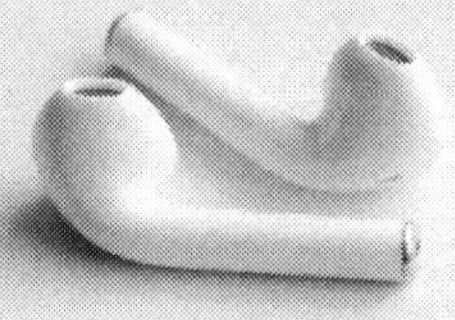

MangoBook Gold

The world is your mango

Rockstar Perks

Join Club Mango

Check out the full webpage here: https://www.johnweiler.co/mango.html

Notice how the design/layout, images and copywriting create a specific feel or experience. Mango's website (similar to Apple's) is in fact a lot like their products: sleek, sexy, visually appealing and minimalistic. The website creates this feeling with an uncluttered, image-heavy design, and ample white space. You'll also notice there is little copywriting on the homepage. This is intentional. Mango doesn't need to sell their product with fancy words, because stunning product design does most of the work.

Now, let's talk about the real Apple for a minute. Since Mango's website is based on theirs, I'd encourage you to check it out: https://www.apple.com/. Doing so will give you a better sense of this type of buying environment.

Either way, Apple's website is a lot like their brick and mortar store. There is lots of space, computers set on pedestals for customers to oooh and ahhh over and a clean layout. Both the website and their stores set the tone for the customer to drop big bucks on premium products.

Now, let's look at a site that's quite the opposite: Trader Joe's. For readers based outside the US, Trader Joe's is a quirky American-based grocery store chain that sells quality food at low prices.

Just like my Mango website above, here's a similar version I've created: Merchant Moe's.

Notice how this site sets an entirely different tone. While the homepage isn't cluttered, it's not as clean and sleek as Apple's: there are smaller images, more text and a layout that, compared to Apple's, is a bit all over the place.

When you look at this homepage, how does it make you feel? For me, the word that comes to mind is "homey." Anyone who has been in a real Trader Joe's store probably gets this vibe. On my Merchant Moe's website there are several specific aspects that create this atmosphere.

The images of food look like they were cooked at home, fresh out of the oven.

Welcome to Merchant Moe's!

Chow Down

8 Delicious Asian Veggies

From India to Japan and everywhere in between, these eight delicious Asian vegetables are sure to whet your appetite.

Bake a Better Baked Potato

When was the last time you had an amazing baked potato? Fear no more. Here's how to up your baked potato game.

How to Win a Food Challenge

The sheer amount of food is mind-boggling. How will you squeeze it all into your stomach? Check out our proven system.

The font choice and graphics also emit this homey feel. The font has an overall dependable, straightforward character and some fonts even seem like they could have been handwritten by your neighbor.

Kitchen Guides

Become a Fry Pan Ninja

Often referred to as the nunchuck of the kitchen (at least by Merchant Moe's CEO), the fry pan can whip up a storm of yummy eats. It's one of the most versatile weapons any chef has at her disposal. Here's how you can learn to wield it like a master and unleash your ultimate cooking genius.

Also, the graphics support this homey characteristic, having an old-fashioned quality to them. Perhaps they remind you a bit of your Grandma's house.

All these little touches are intentional. They set the tone for visitors to buy products while promoting the brand.

Check out the full Merchant Moe's page here: https://www.johnweiler.co/merchantmoe.html

Just like the Apple/Mango example, I encourage you to visit the real Trader Joe's website: https://www.traderjoes.com/home

4 ways to set the tone of your website buying environment

Now that you understand what a website buying environment is, you may wonder how to create yours. Here are four qualities to optimize during your website build:

1. Images: Since websites are visual in nature, this is probably the single biggest way to set the tone. How do your images make potential customers feel? If you're selling medical devices, do the photos look professional and focus solely on the device, or are they grainy and include objects in the background? Do the medical devices look polished and new, or are they covered in dust? The former will increase customer confidence and prep them to buy your products. The latter, grainy and cluttered images, will scare visitors away.

2. Language, word choice: I've written a lot of copy for 5-star hotels in my day. As you can imagine, word choice is critical on these sites. I often use adjectives like "luxurious," "stunning," "breathtaking," "world-class" and so on because visitors who splurge on comfort expect this kind of language. They want the best, so I set that tone with a word choice that prepares them to book a room. You too must know your audience and set the tone with your language. If your website is promoting your gym, use words like "sweat," "toned," "healthy," "fit," "sexy" and so on to prepare the visitor to buy a membership and get ready to experience all those exercise adjectives.

3. Credibility: Important buying environment aspects missing from Trader Joe's and Apple's websites are common credibility indicators. What's a credibility indicator? Things like testimonials, logos of clients and affiliates, awards you've won, etc., that show you're a credible business.

These things are missing because, well, Apple and Trader Joe's don't need them. They're name brands, the latter at least in the US. People already know and trust them, so they don't have to earn confidence with testimonials, endorsements, large social media followings, etc.

You, however, likely do not have the recognition these big companies do (I don't either). That's why it's important to include credibility indicators on your site. Because credibility is a large topic outside the scope of this book, you can learn more about it in Book 1 of the Digital Marketing Success series *Instant Credibility Online.* That said, to get you started, a good way to build trust quickly is to get a logo, ask for testimonials and highlight the number of years you've been in business (as long as it's three or more).

4. Best practices: The last way to establish an irresistible buying environment is to follow today's best website practices. "What are those?" you ask. I'll cover all of them in Your Edge, which follows chapter five of this section.

3.

How many pages? What pages?

You've learned about your website's purpose and buying environments, now let's shift into planning mode. You probably have lots of questions.

What type of content should your website include? How many pages should there be?

Should you go with a massive website like IBM or Apple? Or should you keep it lean like these two by Chris Guillebeau or ClickFunnels?

And once you've decided on the size, what about the type of pages to include?

For business owners, answering this endless list of questions can quickly become a headache.

You'll have a homepage and likely an About page. But besides those, what else? While there's no magical number of pages to include, here are some guidelines I recommend.

Is a bigger website better?

Whether advertising a TV, car or weekend getaway, many marketers will tell you bigger is better. And the Apple and IBM websites may have you nodding in agreement.

However, according to HubSpot (one of the largest marketing technology companies in the world), most people spend less than a minute on any given website. As much as we'd all like to believe droves of visitors will spend endless hours on our sites, eating up our content, captivated by our businesses, it rarely happens.

So should you just create a one-page website?

Years ago, when I worked as a full-time copywriter at a website marketing agency, a coworker and I had a debate about one-page sites. I always liked them because they were easy to write. And, truthfully, I didn't see a problem with them.

But my coworker brought up an interesting counterpoint about their drawbacks. And from that day forward, I've never recommended creating a one-page site. What did my coworker say?

Essentially, he said you don't get a clear understanding of a company in one page.
In my own experience, I tend to agree. I usually haven't learned enough about the business to trust them, which is why an About page is highly recommended. More on that later.

Also, creating a one-page site may lower your chances of ranking in Google's top 10 search results.

Bear in mind, I'm not referring to landing pages, which are often mistaken for one-page sites. For those unfamiliar, a landing page is a sales page that showcases a single product, its benefits and why people should buy it. Landing pages can be extremely effective for selling a single product or service, but they are not the type of websites I'm referring to—they're a different ball game.

Your website page count sweet spot

I always advise clients to start with these four pages: Home, About, Contact and one other page relevant to the business. Of course, if the company needs a larger site, we'll include more. 10 to 15 pages are just fine in my book (though I recommend capping it off there).

Now, you may be wondering, how did I come up with these numbers? Am I pulling them out of thin air? The answer comes back to your website's purpose discussed in Chapter 1.

Remember, the purpose of your website isn't to tell visitors every little detail about your business. Instead, it should tease them into emailing or calling you.

In other words, your website should leave them wanting to know more.

As much as we all love and rave about our businesses (myself included), people on the web want the meat and potatoes. So give them enough information to understand your business and your offer, then answer their other questions when they contact you.

Recommended pages to include

So besides the Home, About and Contact pages, which other pages should you include in your site? And how do you determine those pages?

It all comes back to stepping into your customers' shoes. Think about it. When they visit your website, what do they want to know?

For example, if you're a freelance graphic designer, prospects will likely want to see samples of your past work.

A Portfolio page will inspire confidence and trust in your abilities.

If you're in the legal, accounting or any other service-based industry, then a Services page is a popular choice. Prospects want to learn more about what you offer. You can satisfy this interest via a general Services page or highlight each service separately, like I do on my website below.

For complex or uncommon services, like app development or advertising services, I generally recommend a How It Works page. This page helps prospective clients better understand your service and how it solves their problems.

Other notable pages to include are Testimonials, FAQ and Why Us. These pages either answer questions or demonstrate the value your business provides.

Below is a list of 15 pages I often recommend to clients:

1. Home: Always include.
2. About: Highly recommended as it details your offer and humanizes your business (more on the concept of humanization soon).
3. Contact: Recommended, but you can alternatively add your contact details to every site page.
4. Portfolio: Highly recommended for freelancers.
5. Services: Depending on the complexity or uniqueness of your services.
6. How It Works: Recommended for unfamiliar or complex services.
7. Testimonials: Shows social proof.
8. FAQs: Prospects can find answers faster on this type of page than combing through paragraphs looking for answers scattered across your site.
9. Why Us: Explains why prospects should choose you. Demonstrates how your offer is unique.
10. Blog: Great for SEO and boosting your online presence.
11. Store: For businesses that have products to sell.
12. Partners & Certifications: Shows social proof.
13. Is This You?: If you've read *The Website Homepage Blueprint*, you may remember "Is this you?" as a possible homepage segment. But it can also be a fleshed out inner page that shows prospects you understand them, which can increase sales.
14. Products I Love: A highly recommended page if you offer many affiliate products.

15. Landing page: Worth considering if you're selling a new product or service (note: the page is not titled Landing Page, but is named after the type of product you're selling or the product itself).

Hopefully, this chapter has explained everything you need to know about a website's basic layout. Now, let's talk about inner pages.

4.

Structure of an inner page

You've decided on your website pages and now you're ready to build them. But wait a second. How should their content be structured? Should each be a long scrolling page or a few sentences description?

Typically, I recommend somewhere in between.

But first off, let's define an inner page:

An inner page is every page, minus the homepage.

If the homepage is the front door of your website, everything else is the interior. Think of these inner pages like different rooms in your home. They each have a distinct purpose.

Only include the essentials (most of the time)

Typically you'll want to communicate your point in the fewest words possible. But don't underdo it. Inner pages with only a few sentences rarely provide enough detail to help the visitor.

That said, remember a website is not an opportunity to rave about your awesomeness. Its purpose is focused solely on the customer and how you can help them.

For example, imagine you're an IT services company and have an IT Consulting page. How does this service help customers? Well, your knowledge likely prevents technology headaches and optimizes their networks, which translates into less employee downtime, more productivity and more profits. What business doesn't want that?

The point is, focus on the benefits because that's what visitors want. Just get to those benefits as quickly as possible. Don't ramble. Write about your service in terms of the principle from Chapter 1: how your service helps visitors.

To give you an idea of word count, my inner pages are typically between 150-300 words.

What should an inner page look like?

Believe it or not, you don't necessarily need images on your inner page—sometimes text is enough. That said, avoid big blobs of text, like below:

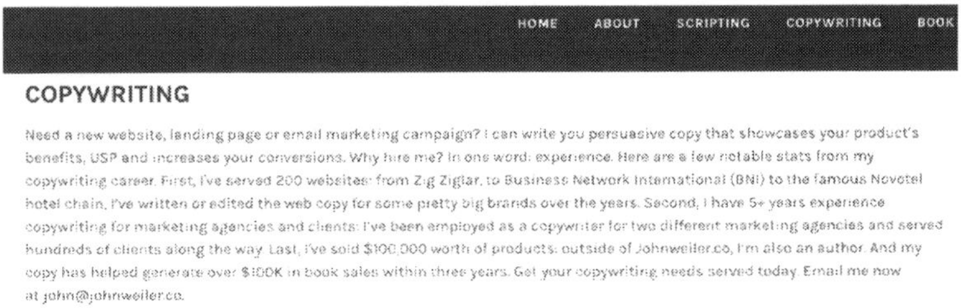

Instead, make your text visually appealing by using block quotes, bullets and headings:

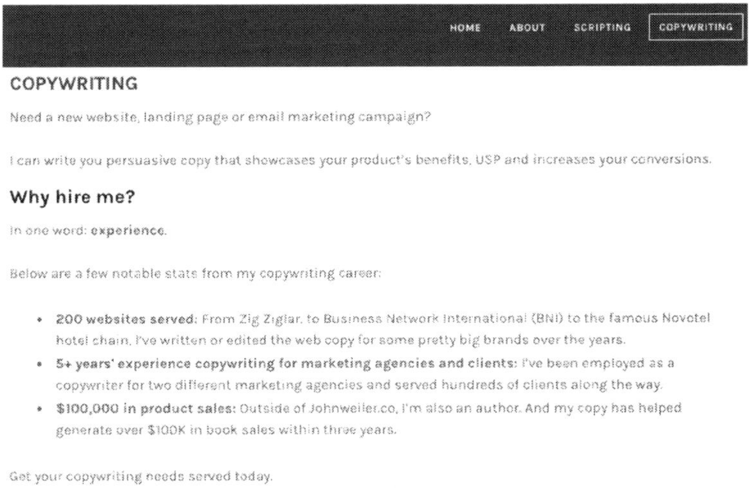

More details on the visual appeal of text in Part 2 of this book.

When it comes to including images, use them only when it makes sense. If you're unsure, remember to look at your business through the eyes of the customer and ask yourself,

"What does the visitor want?" If an image showcases your product or highlights its benefits, then include it.

When should you create a long scrolling inner page?

There's an industry trend to use long scrolling pages, similar to homepages or landing pages, for all your website's inner pages. Instead of communicating your benefits and features in the shortest amount of words, each page is broken into segments and includes detailed copy. To see some examples, check out this landing page for my book An Ordinary Dude's Guide to Meditation or my homepage for johnweiler.co.

While these pages are more visually engaging, there is a fundamental problem with overusing them: your focus is on word count and design, not the visitor.

The choice to use a scrolling page comes back to a core principle of this book: focus on the visitor. If you have a complex service that warrants more details, then by all means, make your service page longer—there are exceptions. A long scrolling page for homepages or landing pages makes sense because you have a lot of information to communicate. But for most inner pages it's unnecessary.

The one thing every inner page needs

Whether the page you build is a long scrolling page or 300-word inner page, it must push visitors to take a specific action.

This is where the call to action (CTA) comes in. A CTA is a button somewhere on the page (there are often multiple throughout a page to catch readers at various opportunities) that tells visitors what to do next. Here are three examples:

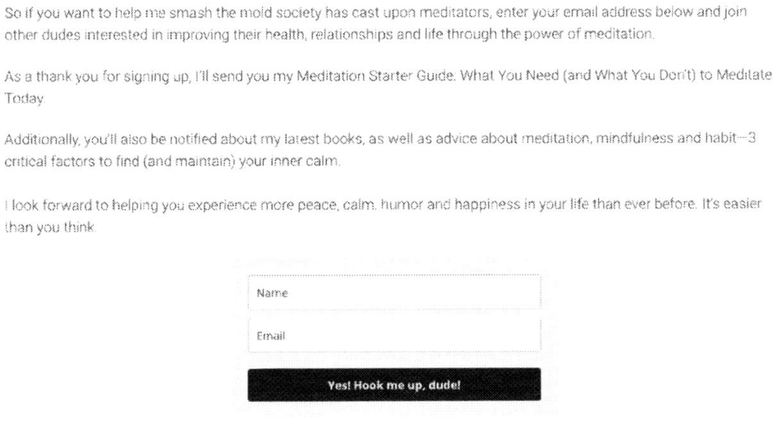

This first example is pretty straightforward. I want visitors to subscribe to my email list, so I give them the chance to say, "Yes! Hook me up, dude!" This is a far more engaging option for my target audience than "Subscribe Now."

In this example from my writer's site, I ask visitors to get in touch. When they click the link, they're brought to my Contact page where they can message or email me.

Not all CTAs need to be big colorful buttons. They can be a link, like in the image above.

As you can see, CTAs guide visitors through your site. They also embody the fundamental point of any website page—have a purpose and spark action, directing visitors where you want them to go and what to do next.

5.

How to write your About page

Your homepage is your website's most visited page, followed by the About page: your second most important page. Just like any page, it has a specific purpose.

3 goals of your About page

While your About page has three goals, it has the same overarching purpose as all pages, which you learned in Chapter 1—promote your brand and show visitors you can help. It does this by first winning their trust and then sharing your unique value. Let's get into the details.

1. Establish Credibility

A crucial aspect of any website is credibility. If visitors think you're an amateur, scammer or get a fishy vibe, they'll bounce. So why should they trust you? Your About page answers that question early, within the first 10 sentences. Notice how I do this on both of my websites.

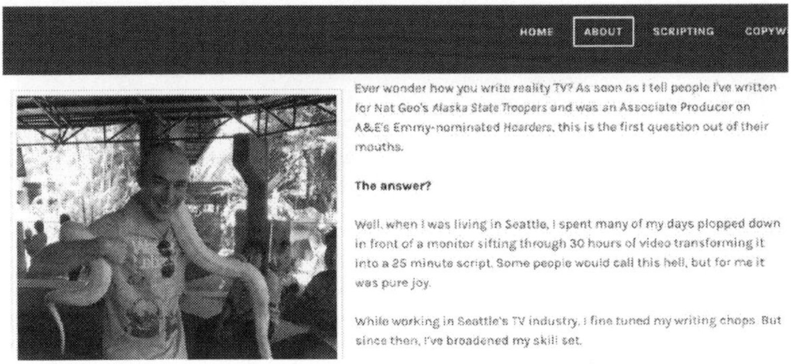

Immediately you notice some recognizable names on johnweiler.co: Nat Geo and A&E. This shows readers that I'm a proven storyteller and my work has been broadcast to millions of viewers. Could an amateur writer do this? Probably not.

Credibility is established differently in the example above: I list the number of years I've been meditating. 15+ isn't something most people can say. If you're a business owner, you can gain credibility using a similar technique. Put the number of years you've been in business somewhere impossible to miss. To learn more about this technique,

I've dedicated an entire chapter to it in *Instant Credibility Online*, but the above example should give you the gist.

Whatever your business sells, provide hard facts, stats or data to prove your credibility. Show—don't tell. Again, you can do this by naming a famous client of yours, the number of years you've been in business or something similar. Just show visitors why they should trust you.

2. Humanize your business

Your About page's next goal is to humanize your business. While I'll discuss this more thoroughly in Part 2 of this book, let's touch on it now. If your visitors feel that they can relate to you or have something in common with you, they'll be more likely to buy from you. Here's how I use that technique in the copywriting of my freelance writing site:

Inside I'm actually terrified. My wife made me take the photo.

Ever wonder how you write reality TV? As soon as I tell people I've written for **Nat Geo's *Alaska State Troopers*** and was an Associate Producer on **A&E's Emmy-nominated Hoarders**, this is the first question out of their mouths.

The answer?

Well, **when I was living in Seattle**, I spent many of my days plopped down in front of a monitor sifting through 30 hours of video transforming it into a 25 minute script. Some people would call this hell, but for me it was pure joy.

While working in Seattle's TV industry, I fine tuned my writing chops. But since then, I've broadened my skill set.

From scriptwriter, to author to copywriter

I've spent far more time traveling than most responsible adults should—**visiting dozens of countries in Asia, Australia and North America**.

I've traveled so much that in 2014 I was compelled to write a book of tips to help 20-somethings get abroad. Little did I know that this first work would eventually kick off my author career—leading to 10 published books that have generated over $100,000 in sales within 3 years. How did I accomplish this?

My copywriting skills and marketing savvy have certainly helped. I've been employed as a Marketing Consultant, Copywriter and Content Director for multiple agencies. And I've invested thousands of dollars in developing my craft, learning from some of the best in the industry—like Carol Tice of Make A Living Writing and Jon Morrow of Smart Blogger.

Today I make a nice passive income from book royalties while I continue to serve my clients' copywriting, scripting and book publishing needs.

Outside the writing world, I'm an **obsessive NBA fanatic and hardcore meditator, practicing meditation and mindfulness for nearly 20 years**.

Notice how I get quite personal above, sharing intimate details about my life. I name a city I lived in (Seattle), TV networks my work has aired on, continents I've traveled to and a few fun facts, like how I enjoy NBA hoops and meditation. Now, chances are, any visitor will share at least one thing in common with me. The NBA is incredibly popular, most people like to travel, a lot of people like meditation and many have heard of Nat Geo and A&E.

What do these details about my life do for the reader?

Here are some of the comments I've gotten from cold prospects:

"Are you a Kobe Bryant fan?"

"I have a brother who lives in Seattle."

"Hoarders was my freakin' favorite show!"

See what's happening here? Readers have formed a connection with me. They feel like they know me and, because of that, I've earned some of their trust. People like working with people they have a connection with, and this is why it's critical to share details about yourself or business on your About page.

Of course, be genuine. Don't make up stuff. I really do love meditation (as you can probably tell from my examples), I'm a huge NBA fan and I travel so much I had one client ask if I'm partially retired. So just put details about your personality out there and visitors will discover things they share in common with you.

Before we move on to the last goal of an About page, there's one more way it can humanize your business: share photos and bios of your employees (assuming you have them). Doing so not only provides visitors more opportunities to form a connection with your staff, but it also illustrates your success. A business with more than one employee subliminally tells website visitors one thing—your business makes money. And a business that makes money can likely produce results, which is something every customer wants.

That said, a solo business isn't a bad thing. It doesn't necessarily mean you aren't making money or aren't trustworthy. And a lot of businesses who hire freelancers know their benefits. My point is, employees are a bonus in the credibility department. So if you have them, flaunt them on your website.

3. Share your USP, benefits or both

The last purpose of an About page is to share your company's USP (unique selling proposition) and/or benefits you offer. If you've never heard of a USP, don't worry. You'll learn all about it in Chapter 7 of this book. For now, just know that a USP is what makes you special. It answers the question, "Why you?" Why should a website visitor choose you over another business?

Inside I'm actually terrified. My wife made me take the photo

Ever wonder how you write reality TV? As soon as I tell people I've written for Nat Geo's *Alaska State Troopers* and was an Associate Producer on A&E's Emmy-nominated *Hoarders*, this is the first question out of their mouths.

The answer?

Well, when I was living in Seattle, I spent many of my days plopped down in front of a monitor sifting through 30 hours of video transforming it into a 25 minute script. Some people would call this hell, but for me it was pure joy.

While working in Seattle's TV industry, I fine tuned my writing chops. But since then, I've broadened my skill set.

From scriptwriter, to author to copywriter

I've spent far more time traveling than most responsible adults should—visiting dozens of countries in Asia, Australia and North America.

I've traveled so much that in 2014 I was compelled to write a book of tips to help 20-somethings get abroad. Little did I know that this first work would eventually kick off my author career—leading to 10 published books that have generated over $100,000 in sales within 3 years. How did I accomplish this?

This is illustrated subtly on my writer site, which mentions my TV and publishing experience. These skills set me apart from most freelancers.

My mission is to change the way people think about the "type of person who meditates" and spread the practice to dudes who would've never tried meditation otherwise.

On my meditation site, the USP is clearly mentioned in my mission: "to change the way people think about the 'type of person who meditates' and spread the practice to dudes who would've never tried meditation otherwise." Benefits—like becoming more calm, peaceful and happy—are also sprinkled throughout the page.

Whether you choose to be straightforward or subtle, be sure to distinguish how your business is unique and, if appropriate, name some benefits you offer.

Your Edge—Design

Now that you have an understanding of web design, let's explore shortcuts to gain an edge over your competitors. As mentioned in this book's Intro, the "Your Edge" sections include strategies to accelerate your results, in terms of leads, profits and conversions. These are the things I wish I knew when I started in digital marketing back in 2012.

3 website design tips to improve conversions

Web design is a complicated and nuanced field. You could spend months getting lost in the weeds or you could focus on a few best practices that generate the biggest improvements:

1. Clean design: 3 critical characteristics

Think back to the buying environments of Mango and Merchant Moe's. Though these sites were different, did you notice how both had a clean design? Neither site was cluttered. Though Merchant Moe's website had more content, both sites made it easy to find what you were looking for fast. They have a clean, professional appearance with solid color backgrounds, crisp images and headings that organize the content.

To build a clean-looking website, I recommend you use all three of those strategies. Let me repeat them below:

- **Solid color backgrounds**: Are important because they improve the readability of your text. A patterned background can be hard on the eyes and distract visitors, which can cause reading difficulty and therefore a bounce. Bonus tip: make your font large and contrast its color with the background. This ensures visitors can easily read your copy.
- **Crisp, beautiful images**: Will give your website a shiny, polished feel. On the flipside, grainy or unfocused images can distract the reader and also damage your business's credibility.
- **Headings:** Organize your content, help visitors understand your value quickly and keep page skimmers happy.

2. Simple design: A classic marketing technique

Along with a clean design, did you notice how simple Mango and Merchant Moe's websites were? Neither is fancy. They get to the point, communicate the essentials and include simple, clear headlines to help visitors navigate the page.

Simplicity is a deliberate design strategy and a timeless marketing tactic. It's even mentioned in the Heath brothers' excellent marketing book *Made to Stick* as one of the six characteristics of memorable content. So keep your website simple. You'll reduce bounce rates as you provide a clear, easy path for visitors to take your desired action (subscribe, contact you, etc.). Less is more.

3. Purpose: How to use your website's theme to guide your design

My wife often thinks I'm a genius when it comes to decoding a movie's purpose. I can pick apart any film and pinpoint its message: the purpose of individual scenes, and whether or not the movie does a good job of illustrating its theme.

It's not a gift, but a result of nearly two decades of studying storytelling. Between working in the TV industry, earning a degree in film and dissecting movies with award-winning friends who work at Pixar and BuzzFeed, I know what makes a story engaging. The reason I bring this up?

The most important part of any movie, which determines a story's quality, is the theme. The theme is the core message of a movie. It unlocks a film's true purpose and allows you to objectively judge its story, without getting lost in opinions. Contrary to popular belief, a theme isn't one word, like "water," "determination" or "happiness." A theme is a sentence.

For example, let me share the themes of two movies I recently saw: *It* and *Arrival.* The theme of *It* is "Fear can only hurt you if you allow it to." The *Arrival* theme is "Language shapes your perspective and can open your mind to new possibilities."

Each scene in these movies has a purpose that helps illustrate their themes. And the same goes for your website. Each page, each sentence, each image also has a theme or purpose. How do you figure yours out? Let me show you:

My website helps visitors because ________

Just fill in the blank. Each detail of your website, from your homepage banner to images and the layout of your copy, must follow whatever theme you wrote.

Some examples of what you could write are, my website helps visitors because:

- I offer unique life coaching services, advice and a community
- My social media marketing services get results

- I take care of my clients' IT headaches so they don't have to

Notice how all these themes are pretty broad and somewhat vague. That's okay. Your website copy will dig into the details. It will answer questions for the website visitor, like, "What makes your life coaching services and advice unique?," "What kind of results have your social media services produced?," "How do you alleviate my IT headaches?"

In other words, the broad theme is used as a guideline that directs the content you create.

The key point here is twofold: use the theme to guide your content and always look at your website through the visitors' eyes. Is it helping them? Does it show how your business can make a difference in their lives or solve their problems? Does it ask them to take action?

Don't worry, if you struggle with the idea of stepping into your customers' shoes, the next part of this book will help.

Part II

Copywriting: Hypnotize your website visitors

Great copywriting can seem hypnotic. It flows smoothly. Captures readers' imaginations. And stirs up their emotions. The techniques you'll learn in this section are designed to do just that—they focus on the visitor, zone in on their unique desires and demonstrate why your product or service is the best fit for them.

Just like in Part I of this book, you need to let go of your urge to brag about your business. Because it's not about you. Copywriting is really about tapping into your customers' psyches and showing that you understand them. Understanding and empathy is how you win trust.

In this section, we'll cover four critical copywriting principles:

- The word "you"
- USPs
- Humanize your business
- Sell the end result

In the "Your Edge" section, we'll also get into my three favorite copywriting techniques I use in almost all copy I write.

Lastly, you'll learn how to write copy for the web. While this may not sound as sexy as the above techniques, it's absolutely critical in today's world where everyone is glued to their phone. You'll learn about bullets, block paragraphs, sentence length, readability and other copywriting techniques that focus on how the words look on a web page.

So, without further ado, let's get the ball rolling, starting with one of my favorite words…

6.

Start with YOU

Remember the marketing paradox shift from Part 1 of this book? Let's return to that concept again.

Copywriting should rarely highlight how cool you or your product are, but rather what your product does for the buyer. When you understand this, you stop looking at the customer through the eyes of your product, and start looking at your product through the eyes of your customers.

If you haven't done so already, one of the most effective ways to improve your website copy is to sprinkle the word "you" in as much as possible.

Reading the word "you" is like hearing your name, which research has shown activates unique parts of the brain and, according to famous marketer Neil Patel, has a hypnotic effect on readers.

I personally love the word "you" and even had a former marketing boss gush about how John's favorite word is "you." Have you noticed how much I use the word in this book? If you haven't yet, you will in the coming pages.

How can you get more “you” into your writing?

Let me show you with some sample copy for an imaginary brewery, below. Let’s start with the version focused more on the business, instead of the customer:

We sell a variety of beers at our brewery. We have porters, blondes, stouts, IPAs and many more that our brew master has crafted. We also offer customized six packs, where our customers can mix and match their favorite beers to their heart’s desire.

Now let’s look at the same copy, but focused on “you,” the customer. Changes are in BOLD:

You can taste *a variety of beers at our brewery.* ***If you like*** *porters, blondes, stouts* ***or*** *IPAs, our brew master has crafted* ***these*** *and many more* ***for you to indulge in****.* ***What’s more, you can also*** *customize* ***your very own*** *six pack.* ***You read that correctly. You can*** *mix and match* ***your*** *favorite beers to* ***your*** *heart's desire.*

See how changing a few words makes the copy more pleasant and engaging to read? Swap out “we” and “their” for “you” and slightly adjust the sentences.

Now, there isn’t a science to this. I don’t think it’s fair to say there’s a proven ratio of how many “you” there should be compared to “I” or “we.” That said, a rough estimate would maybe be 80% "you" and 20% "I," "our" or "their."

Forming the habit of writing more "you" into your copy is difficult at first. I remember how awkward the above exercise was when I first tried it a decade ago. But it gets easier with time. Today, adding "you" into my copy is second nature and I rarely think about it, except for moments like now when I'm teaching. Stick with this habit long enough, and it will become the same for you.

7.

Know your USP

When it comes to copywriting, and marketing in general, knowing your USP is crucial.

A USP is **what makes your product special.** Why would a customer buy your product over that of a competitor?

To explain this concept, let me share a story.

A marketing company owner once told me his USP was that he offered world-class content, all of which was produced in-house. Now, let me ask you this. How special do you think "in-house content creation" and "world-class content" are?

With the exception of very few cases, "in-house content creation" and calling your content "world-class" are not USPs. Here's why.

In-house content creation is common among agencies. And if it's common, then it's not special. I mean, why should the customer buy your in-house content when 10 other businesses can do the same?

I mentioned exceptions. And that could happen if it was widely known that all marketing agencies in town outsourced their content creation. In that unlikely case, then yes, this could be considered a USP.

Calling your content world-class causes a similar problem. Essentially, this word is a meaningless label, kind of like in the movie *Elf* where a restaurant proclaims they have the "World's best cup of coffee." Or how food companies label their supposedly healthy cookies or crackers as "natural." No law governs the use of these words or phrases. Anyone can say them, just like anyone can say their content is world-class.

Now if the content was truly world-class, would it be a USP? It would and it wouldn't. Come again? Well, as mentioned anyone can use the word. So competitors could easily proclaim that their content is world-class too. Therefore, saying your content is, doesn't really make it special. What I recommend doing instead is to dig deeper and ask yourself, "**Why** is the content world-class?"

Has it won awards? Do you employ a famous writer or designer who creates it? A "yes" to either of these questions may differentiate your content as world-class. More on this **why** concept in a bit, but for now let's look at some examples, starting with the true USP of the aforementioned marketing company.

4 real life USP examples: From Amazon, Apple, a marketing company and yours truly

Now if world-class content and in-house content creation was not the company's USP, then what was? Well, there was something special about this business.

It was their Facebook marketing system, which worked as follows. Each day the same Facebook users were served a different form of content via ads, anything from a video on Monday, to an article on Tuesday, an infographic on Wednesday and so on. While you may not think this marketing technique is unique, no competing agencies in town, and possibly the country, were doing it. The system was special and, importantly, was incredibly effective at wrangling leads and sales for clients. This system was the company's real USP.

Let's look at a few more examples:

The USP for my business Ordinary Dude Mediation is pretty much in the title: meditation for dudes. Now, what does that actually mean? Let me show you with an example from my site:

As you can see, the banner copy provides an all-inclusive message, specifically naming a few demographics typically shunned by the meditation community: atheists and beer drinkers. These people can benefit from meditation as much as anyone. And judging from the 10,000+ books I've sold on the topic, there is a market here.

I should note that your USP must be true. In addition to meditating for nearly 20 years, I am also a beer drinker. And though I'm not an atheist (I'm agnostic), the style of meditation I teach is not meant to improve your life spiritually, but rather your quality of life.

This USP, again, works because very few people cater to this market. It gives potential readers a reason to choose me over the thousands of other meditation books and teachings out there.

Next up is Apple.

You could say their USP is: The most user-friendly, sleek and durable IT products.*

Wait a second, didn't I just tell you to avoid generalizations, like "user-friendly," "sleek" and "durable"? I did. But, here's the thing, Apple doesn't say their USP, they **show it**. You see it in their store design, websites, computers and other gadgets. And most people would agree Apple offers the most user-friendly computer products around. While their durability may not be as widely known, if you're an Apple user, you can probably attest to their products' reliability. I generally get six to eight years out of my laptops, Mac minis and iPhones, with few if any problems.

Last is a brand you're likely familiar with: Amazon.

Amazon is the Walmart of the internet. Which is not surprising, since Jeff Bezos was enamored with Sam Walton, Walmart's founder.

While many people may think Amazon doesn't have a USP, just ask yourself, where else can you get the cheapest products online with such a wide selection and fast shipping?

You guessed it, that's their USP: Wide selection, cheap products, fast shipping.*

Amazon does this better than anyone. In fact, they're so good, I know many people who hate Amazon, but continue to shop there because of the convenience, speed and low pricing. In other words, Amazon's USP is so strong that it sucks customers in like a magnet. This is what you should aim for with your USP. Create such an advantage that prospective customers find it difficult to ignore you.

The 5 Whys

You may have heard of The 5 Whys before, a concept developed by the car manufacturer Toyota last century. While the technique was originally used as a way to identify a problem's root cause, it also works wonderfully in copywriting. And I'd highly recommend using it to discover your USP. How does it work?

Every time you name your USP, ask yourself "Why?" Do so five times until you get to the heart of it.

It'll be easier to understand with an example. So let's go through this process now, with the word "world-class." If I was to hypothetically use The 5 Whys to uncover a business owner's USP (in this example, let's call him Tom) here's what it would look like.

So Tom, what makes your business special?

1. We have world-class content.

Why is it world-class?

2. Because we have experienced writers.

Why are they experienced?

3. Because they've been writing professionally for a total of 50+ years.

What have they written about in those five plus decades?

4. All kinds of things, from books to TV shows and articles published in magazines.

Anything notable that makes them world-class?

5. One writer is a New York Times bestselling author, another is a regular Forbes contributor and a third has written shows for ABC, Fox and HGTV.

See how The 5 Whys can uncover the nitty gritty details of your USP?

Number 3 (writing professionally for a total of 50+ years) is a good USP in and of itself and probably should be included in the marketing copy, but the 2 extra Whys really explain why the writing is world-class. Obviously, the last two questions don't begin with why, but you get the point: keep asking questions, at least five times, until you uncover the real USP.

Does your customer see your USP immediately?

This is important. Your USP should be one of the first things a customer sees upon visiting your website, so I recommend including it in your homepage's main banner copy. Doing so can spark visitors' interest, enticing them to spend more time on your website learning about your offer.

Generally, the USP should be conveyed in the first touchpoint a prospect has with your business—whichever form that takes. In your advertising, brochures or landing pages, highlight your USP in copy and images. If a prospect asks about your business at a networking event, keep your response short, to-the-point and focused on the USP.

Your USP is a hook. It can pique interest and eventually transform a prospect into a customer.

*I'm not sure if either Amazon or Apple have ever publicized their USPs. These are my interpretations of them based on my own observations.

8.

Humanize your business

One of the hardest things to do online is prove you're a legitimate company. Scammers and unethical business owners plague digital marketplaces and are constantly finding new ways to swindle innocent targets.

How can you prove you're a relatable, good-hearted business owner who offers valuable products or services?

You need to humanize your business. Remember that concept from Part 1? Here's a reminder in case you forgot...

To humanize your business is to reveal the human aspect of your website, brand or online presence. The customer must sense that real, relatable people are running your organization. In other words, be transparent. Give customers a behind-the-scenes look inside your business, share personal details about yourself and employees and basically just be human. Here are some ways to do that.

4 ways to humanize your business

1. Give behind-the-scenes access with video

One of the best ways to humanize your business is to shoot a behind-the-scenes video of your company's office and staff.

If you've read *Instant Credibility Online*, you already know a high-quality video does two things: it proves real people work at your business and your company has money and likely paying clients. Video has the appearance of being expensive (even though some can be produced for less than $1,000) and subtly tells viewers that you're willing to associate your face with your product (very few scammers can pull that off).

Outside the behind-the-scenes format, almost any video style that features your staff and offices will do wonders for humanizing your business. You could shoot something as simple as your employees talking about your product, service or business and how it adds value to customers.

2. Share you and your employees' hobbies

We discussed this in Chapter 5, but it's worth mentioning again. On your About page, name you and your staff's hobbies. Doing so creates a warm connection between your business and prospects. What's a warm connection? For those who haven't read *Instant Credibility Online* or *The Website Homepage Blueprint*, here's how I define the term.

A warm connection is common interests or similarities you or staff members share with prospects that create a bond. In addition to my NBA fanatic example from Chapter 5, I often connect with customers over my love of meditation. Just like basketball, prospects have even brought up this hobby of mine on our first call. In other words, they read about the hobbies on my website or saw me mention them online and felt compelled to share their similar interests. The relationship was warming up before we had even spoken to each other.

3. Showcase client and affiliation logos

While logos scream volumes for your credibility, they can also create a warm connection. I regularly recommend my clients to showcase logos of their own clients, affiliations or partners on their website. Just like hobbies, when prospects see you're affiliated with a familiar brand, a connection is created instantly.

For example, if they're friends with the owner of their local burger joint and see you're partners, they'll be happier to work with you. To the prospect, it will feel like she already knows you because she knows Sam, the burger joint owner. It's friendship by association. And this warm connection is the equivalent of earning a little bit of trust that you can leverage to win the prospect's business.

4. Share pictures of yourself, staff and office

We discussed pictures briefly in Chapter 5, but I want to reemphasize their importance and provide a few more tips. Just like video, pictures of yourself, staff and offices humanize your business.

Whenever possible, avoid stock photos and use real pictures of your company. Stock photos can be used by anyone. They're impersonal, lack uniqueness and can raise questions about your business's authenticity. So if you have the budget, hire a professional photographer to shoot pictures of your team. It will be a worthwhile investment for your website and online presence.

Customers want to work with professionals: 3 ways to show you are one

Customers not only want to deal with real people, but also professionals that offer a legitimate, helpful service. When most people think of a professional, they probably think of someone in a suit and tie with a nice haircut. But that's not what I mean at all. You can sell thousands of products in jeans and a t-shirt while talking about your love of beer, just as I've done with Ordinary Dude Meditation.

My point is, professionalism online isn't necessarily about the appearance of you as a person, but rather the appearance of your website. For example, the small details below are important:

1. URL: Companies with a .wix.com or .wordpress.com URL scream unprofessionalism. If the business won't even invest $20 per year in a legitimate URL, how can they provide quality products or services? Https is another small, subtle sign. Without it, your visitors may see a warning that says "This website is not secure" before loading your content. That could put a serious dent in your trustworthiness.

2. Logo: Like your URL, a logo is a subtle sign that reveals your professionalism. That's not to say a scammer can't have a logo (they obviously can), but going the extra mile to create one provides a credibility boost as many new businesses forgo this step.

3. Favicon: For those unfamiliar with this term, you've likely seen thousands of favicons before. They're the little icons, similar to a company's logo, in the upper left corner of browser tabs.

You can do well without a favicon (I worked for a small marketing company that didn't have a favicon for a few years). But if a prospect notices your Wix or WordPress favicon, your chances of a bounce have increased. So be sure to ask your designer to create your favicon in the same package as your logo.

9.

Think like a designer—Secrets of the written word

Writers write. Designers design.

There's nothing more to it, right? Each expert sticks to their specialized role.

Obviously, writers are better at writing than designers (and vice versa). But adopting a design mentality when you write copy for your website can help you avoid common digital marketing pitfalls:

1. Web content overload: According to MarketingProfs, two million blog posts are published each day. As for new websites, estimates range from 70,000 to 140,000+ launched per day.
2. Online content is hard on the eyes: More specifically, reading from screens tends to cause eye strain for many.

So, how does thinking like a designer solve these problems?

Well, designers are experts at making information look pretty, easy-to-read and engaging. All things you can do with your web copy.

How to write readable web copy

Are you old enough to remember what websites looked like in the mid-2000s? Most of the time, you had to slog through pages of unbroken text that could've been mistaken for a car manual. A sort of digital natural selection emerged and the easiest pages to read performed better than the rest. Let's take a look at what they did to catch readers' eyes.

Bullets

Bullet point lists help you pack more information into fewer words and add visual variety to your writing—which skimmers love. Take this example from my website's Copywriting page.

Why hire me?

In one word: **experience**.

Below are a few notable stats from my copywriting career:

- **200 websites served:** From Zig Ziglar, to Business Network International (BNI) to the famous Novotel hotel chain, I've written or edited the web copy for some pretty big brands over the years.
- **5+ years' experience copywriting for marketing agencies and clients:** I've been employed as a copywriter for two different marketing agencies and served hundreds of clients along the way.
- **$100,000 in product sales:** Outside of Johnweiler.co, I'm also an author. And my copy has helped generate over $100K in book sales within three years.

See how easily you can absorb the bullet points? Even if you don't read all the content, you'll almost automatically read "Why hire me?" and then the bolded, bulleted answers: "200 websites served," "5+ years' experience copywriting for marketing agencies and clients," "$100,000 in product sales."

I highly recommend you do the same and include a quick, bold phrase at your bullet point's beginning. This phrase should highlight a benefit, USP or hint at what the bullet's content is about.

In other words, it will quickly communicate your value and/or get the visitor to keep reading.

Headings

You'll notice almost all websites use headings to make content easier to digest, similar to how I've done in this book.

A long block of text is overwhelming. But when it's suddenly broken down into small chunks, it makes the content more manageable and again, easy to read.

Homepage or inner page headings should serve one of a few purposes: explain what the content is about, hint at what it's about or name the benefit of reading that section.

In most cases, I recommend the hinting tactic because it builds curiosity—which is the most likely way to pique your readers' interest and keep them reading.

Block paragraphs

These days almost everyone writes in block paragraphs on the web. And of course, I advise you to do the same.

But how long should block paragraphs be?

It depends on two factors: the form of the copy and the audience reading it.

The form is whether the content is an article, blog post, page of your website or landing page. For articles, blog posts and some landing pages, I recommend keeping your blocks short and varying them in length, much like I do in this chapter.

Just like with headings, breaking up blogs or articles into smaller blocks of text (one to five lines) makes the content easier to read and less overwhelming. And varying the length of these blocks gives your content a much more visual appeal. For example, check out the block paragraphs for this article I wrote for ordinarydudemeditation.com:

The middle way. This buddhist philosophy is all about living a life in between the extremes.

Buddha himself was born a prince and lived a luxurious life within palace walls in southern Nepal. In his late 20's, he left this life behind him and later followed asceticism, which is a self-discipline that rejects worldly pleasures in pursuit of spiritual goals. During this period of his life, Buddha starved himself and eventually became so weak he nearly died.

The remains of Buddha's palace in southern Nepal

He eventually wised up and realized that living a life of either extreme—luxury or self denial—doesn't get you any closer to enlightenment. Either lifestyle can cloud your vision. It's best to live somewhere in between.

Now, the middle way in no way mentioned that drinking beer is okay on the path to enlightenment and mental clarity.

But Ordinary Dude Meditation is not about Buddhism.

However, us ordinary dudes can learn from this story and apply the principle of the middle way to our lives. As beer drinking meditators, we can enjoy our adult beverages and still reap the benefits

As you can see, block paragraphs vary in length from one to four lines.

Now to my second point: audience. If you're selling an expensive, high-end product to an upscale audience, use longer blocks of text—even as long as 10 lines.

The reason is, short text blocks are generally conversational and casual. When you're selling a $10 book, there isn't much risk to the buyer, so adopting a conversational tone is appropriate.

But if you're selling a $10,000 product that could make or break your buyer's business, when there's considerable financial risk, do you think the buyer wants to be spoken to casually? I wouldn't. Casual is good, but not if you're selling expensive products that pose a high risk to the buyer.

Depending on the target audience, blocks of website text generally range from one to eight lines. So when it comes to short or long text blocks, here's a quick breakdown of when to use each...

Longer

- Purpose: Reveals your professionalism and/or speaks to a more upscale audience
- Tone: Professional
- Form: Website pages, landing pages (but depends on the audience)
- Length: 3-10 lines
- Risk to buyer: Higher risk

Shorter

- Purpose: Humanizes your business. Makes you appear more relatable.
- Tone: Casual, conversational
- Form: Blog posts, articles, landing pages (but depends on the product)
- Length: 1-5 lines
- Risk to buyer: Low to moderate risk for buyers

Bear in mind, this isn't a science. These are just basic guidelines to show how the length of text blocks illustrate your brand's personality.

Color and style of the text

Last but not least, the color and font of your website's text is crucial. Yes, really. This advice may sound unbelievable, but if you get these two elements wrong, you can follow every guideline in this book to the letter and fail to get a single lead.

So what's the perfect color and font for your website text?

No, it's not blue, green, white or even black. No, it's not Helvetica, Futura or Times New Roman. The actual answer has nothing to do with a specific color or font. Instead, it has to do with the text's readability and how well it contrasts with the website's background color. Let's discuss both these points:

Readability: One of the most important, and often understated, elements of your website is readability. How easy is your text to read? Not only does color matter, but so does font choice. Fancy, highly stylized fonts can be difficult to read. And if your words aren't easily readable, it will affect your sales—guaranteed. People don't have time to squint at your web copy to try and decipher your message because you chose a cursive font with a pastel color. They will bounce. So make sure your font is readable. If you're unsure of which to go with, some of my favorites include Arial, Courier and Baskerville.

Contrast: Again, the specific color you choose for your website is not nearly as important as how well that text contrasts with the website background. For example, red text on a brown background will be hard to see. As will yellow text on a white background. Always think about contrast. No matter if it's the color of your words, the color of your logo or a book cover, contrast draws the eye by making particular images stand out.

Varying the sentence length is crucial

This applies not just to web copywriting, but copywriting in general. Vary your sentence length. If all your sentences are the same length, the writing sounds monotonous. Here's an example.

Today is a good day for several reasons. At work your boss gave you a promotion. Also, your wife finally got pregnant. And another plus is your brother got engaged. But then you got news your dog was hit by a car. You feel devastated and your world is turned upside down.

Are you bored yet?

Okay, let's try this again, varying the sentence length.

Today is a good day. You got a promotion, your wife finally got pregnant and your brother is now engaged. But then it happened. You got news your dog was hit by a car. Your heart is crushed, and suddenly your world is turned upside down. You're devastated.

While you'll likely agree the second paragraph is more engaging, there's another takeaway here. Notice how short the first sentence is, "Today is a good day." This is intentional.

From Joe Sugarman to Jon Morrow, many legendary copywriters have hailed the importance of a short first sentence. Why?

It's easy to read.

People love easy (myself included). Whether you're purchasing a product, ordering delivery or opting for Netflix instead of going out, people are more likely to complete an easy task than a hard one. So when you keep the first sentence short, it sucks the reader into your copy. It's so easy to read they almost read the second sentence automatically.

A short, four-word sentence is as unavoidable as reading a stop sign is. As soon as your eyes come across one, your brain processes the short message instantly. It's almost as if you have no choice but to read it.

Ready to improve your web copy?

Next time you write web copy, try thinking like a designer.

Try to look at the text without actually reading it. Just keep your gaze wide and ask yourself, "Do certain points stick out? Does it look easy to read? Do the length of sentences and block paragraphs vary?"

Without actually reading the copy, how does it look visually on the page?

Does it feel overwhelming? Or do you feel bored just looking at it?

Think about it. Analyze your writing as a whole and ask yourself, "How can I make this better?"
If you do that, you're more likely to get your copy read, engage your readers and sell some products.

10.

Transformations, identity and selling the result

The copywriting industry has an old saying: customers don't buy the drill, but the hole the drill produces. In the same vein, I often say artists don't buy the paintbrush, but the possibilities it allows: painting a stunning work of art that may someday hang in a museum, leading to world fame and riches.

People buy the result—they buy the outcome the product produces.

For this reason, selling the transformation and an identity are two powerful copywriting techniques. Let's talk about them.

Sell the Transformation: How will your product change the customer?

While all customers want the result a product produces, that result can vary. Sometimes it's simple, like the drill example or a sleeping pill, which could produce a good nap or a sound night's sleep.

However, selling a transformation emphasizes a bigger, more dramatic change. It's something that will take time, effort and perseverance, but can overwhelmingly transform the life of the customer for the better. This is why it excites buyers—the transformation is the result on steroids. The best way to illustrate this concept is with examples.

Couchto5K: Invented by Josh Clark in the mid '90s, this program transforms the average couch potato into a 5K runner within 9 weeks. Not surprisingly, the program went viral with its catchy name, which highlights the participant's journey. It's helped transform over five million people to this day.

20booksto50K: A popular community in the author world, the name was coined by Michael Anderle, one of the group's founders. He predicted if he could write 20 books, he'd earn 50K a year, which would allow him to retire in Mexico. Just like the Couchto5K example, 20booksto50K reveals the journey a person makes to the result: 50K a year.

Nobody to influencer: This phrase is in the subtitle of my popular book *Instant Credibility Online: 25 tactics to win website visitors' trust. And go from nobody to influencer in 6 months or less*. Being a copywriter, I really wanted to sell the transformation this book could produce. So I added it into the subtitle, which is one of the reasons for the book's success: it's sold 5,000+ copies, hit the Amazon bestseller list a few dozen times, and landed me multiple podcast appearances.

6 figure yoga teacher: This was a book title I brainstormed for a client who helps yoga teachers reach six figures. The original title I believe was *How to be a successful yoga teacher or studio owner*. The latter is obviously not specific. What does "successful" mean? Talking with the client, it was clear that six figures was the result students desired and that she could deliver. So the new title was obvious. Sell the transformation: become a six figure yoga teacher.

These examples illustrate how you can sell the transformation. Remember, it's about the big dramatic change you can produce. The next tactic is similar, but focuses more on the instant result your customers get when they buy from you.

The Aspirational Identity: Who do your customers become when they buy your product?

An Aspirational Identity is a concept I first learned from Donald Miller, author of the hit book *Building A Story Brand.* The term represents who the customer wishes or aspires to be.

In other words, when customers buy a product that touts an aspirational identity, they immediately join a group or subculture. Just like selling the transformation, the best way to understand the concept is through examples:

Patagonia - The thoughtful, environmentally conscious outdoors person

If you're unfamiliar with Patagonia, it's an outdoor clothing and equipment company that emphasizes social and environmental responsibility. One percent of their profits go towards preserving and protecting the environment, and the company is transparent about where and how their products are made. By purchasing their gear, you immediately join a group of socially and environmentally responsible outdoors people—which is the aspirational identity Patagonia sells.

Gerber knives - Tough guys doing tough things

This example is from an instructional video by Donald Miller in which he discussed how buying a Gerber pocket knife boosted his self-esteem. Which made him question, what is the aspirational identity being sold? The answer was "tough guys doing tough things." By buying that pocket knife, Miller immediately became, or at least felt, a bit tougher and perhaps a little more manly.

An Ordinary Dude's Guide to Enlightenment - Beer drinkin' dudes can be enlightened, too

When I launched this book in 2019, sales were disappointing. The product page's original opening line was, "This ain't your grandpa's enlightenment." I thought it was fun, but it clearly missed the mark as initial sales sucked. I figured the problem had to be the copy. So taking Donald Miller's advice, I switched the opening line to "Beer drinkin' dudes can be enlightened, too" and suddenly sales exploded, going from about 5 a day to 30 a day (an increase of 600%) for the last 3 days of my launch. The aspirational identity made it clear that you don't have to be a hippie or a spiritual person to seek enlightenment, you can just be a beer drinkin' dude.

The key difference between Selling the Transformation and Aspirational Identity is time. Both tactics sell the result, but the time it takes to achieve said result varies. Sell the Transformation is a journey while the Aspirational Identity is immediate.

As you can see, both copywriting tactics are incredibly powerful. People want the result. They want to change or belong to a group. So tell them who they'll become once they buy your product.

Your Edge—Copywriting

You now have a solid foundation of web copywriting knowledge. But besides the Start with You, Sell the Transformation and Aspirational Identity techniques, I haven't shared too many specific copywriting tactics.

The truth is there are hundreds of copywriting techniques out there. This book's purpose isn't to give a lesson in all or even most of them, but instead provide a shortcut to the most important ones.

3 best ways to write copy that sells

In my years of copywriting experience, the three techniques I use most often, that make the most difference in my sales are as follows:

1. Sell the Dream

Just like in last chapter's discussion on Sell the Transformation and Aspirational Identity, Sell the Dream also sells the result. However, this technique is much more fluid.

Think of Aspirational Identity and Sell the Transformation as a photograph you place in your prospect's head. Sell the

Dream is more than a single frame, it's an entire movie. Which is more memorable?

Most people can remember their favorite films easily. Their favorite photographs or paintings are more difficult. With Sell the Dream, you're essentially creating a mental movie of exactly what your reader wants. And that's powerful.

Take a boat for example. If someone buys a boat, yes, they literally buy a vessel that floats on the water. But that's not their real interest. What they really want are the warm, sunny days spent on its deck. Knocking back beers with their buddies and wives as they eat hot dogs, watching their kids splash in the water to the sound of the summer's hottest new Taylor Swift song blaring from the radio.

That is the dream. It's the fantasy your customers imagine your product will give them and what they really desire, not the product itself. To Sell the Dream, you must know your customers' true interests. What do they want? What are their hopes and dreams? Why do they buy your product?

If you can answer these questions, you can put their dream in writing and use fantasy-like imagery to sell your product or service.

2. Smack em' with a spellbinding dose of emotion

Emotion is one of the most powerful forces on earth. It creates a lot of good, driving billions of dollars a year in charitable donations, anniversary gifts and crowdfunding campaigns. And also bad, causing people to kill, lie, cheat and do despicable things.

Beyond driving people to do things in the heat of the moment that they could never imagine themselves doing, emotions also linger. If you've had a blowout argument with your spouse, you know calming down can be an hour-long or even day-long process.

In copywriting and sales, emotion can be used to your advantage. If you can make people feel something, you can spark their emotions into a sale. While selling the dream paints an emotional picture of customers' desires, particular word choices can also produce emotions.

Jon Morrow offers a brilliant list of power words that I use regularly in my writing. Words like "breathtaking," "cesspool," "triumph" and "skyrocket."

When you read these words, you feel them in your gut. A word like "majestic" may give you a sense of wonder, "dumb" might make you cringe and "outrage" may fill you with anger.

Now, one word alone likely won't be enough to transform a lead into a buyer. But stacking these words in your Sell the Dream description can.

As mentioned, I used to write a lot of copy for 5-star hotels. Check out all the power words (in bold) I used when describing a wedding package.

Your ***special*** *day is* ***once-in-a-lifetime****. Imagine exchanging your* ***vows*** *and* ***proclaiming*** *your* ***undying love*** *for each other atop of Bangkok's highest skyscraper. As you* ***sweetly kiss*** *your* ***soulmate's lips*** *and say "I do," you'll be surrounded by* ***best friends, family*** *members, and* ***loved ones*** *on the* ***top of the world****, nearly touching the* ***heavens****...*

Look at how the power words or power phrases are stacked on top of each other. For your target readers, in this case brides-to-be, doing so creates feelings and visuals in their minds that overpower rational thinking. They become caught up in their own emotion, fantasizing about the dream that awaits them once they buy. When combined like this, power words can be a compelling force that transforms prospects into customers.

3. Highlight the USP

Last of my holy trinity of copywriting techniques is something we discussed extensively in this section of the book—USPs. Assuming you read Chapter 7, there's not much else you need to know. Except...where on your website do you mention your USP?

Just like the Start with You tactic, there's no science to it. You can put your USP anywhere and everywhere. Obviously, don't overdo it. But whenever it makes sense, feel free to slip your USP into your copy because it's a major selling point.

All that said, a few places are more ideal for your USP than others. As mentioned earlier, your homepage's main banner is one of them. To see an example, flip back to Chapter 7 and check out Ordinary Dude Meditation's banner, which illustrates this strategy.

Headlines, in general, are the best places to name your USP because many prospects will skim through your website. Make your USP big in a headline, and they're much more likely to read it as it's highly visible.

Another great place for your USP is in your homepage's USP section. What's that? It's a homepage segment focused entirely on what makes your business special. Let's check out an example, also from Ordinary Dude Meditation:

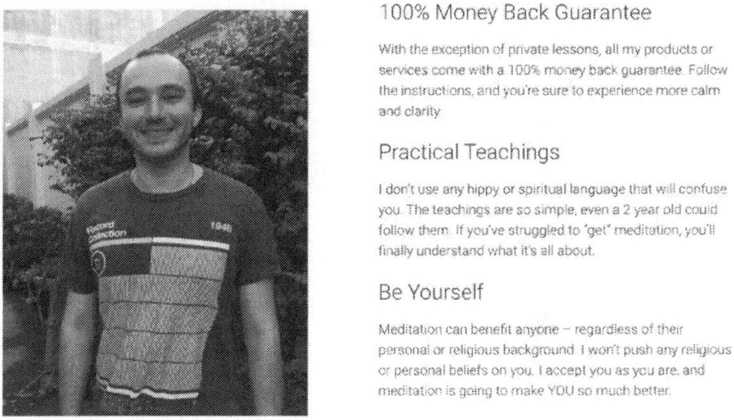

The USP is flaunted, naming why you should choose me over other meditation teachers: money back guarantee, you can be yourself and practicality. Consider a USP section for your own website because it really draws attention to why prospects should choose your business.

If you'd like to know more about USP sections, I dedicate an entire chapter to it in Book 2 of this series, *The Website Homepage Blueprint*.

Part III

Marketing: The myth of instant inbound leads

We've come a long way in this book. You've learned about the purpose of a website, the characteristics of an attractive website and how to write sales copy that converts.

Before we go further, let me share a little website industry secret. Even if you write the sexiest web copy and design a high converting, visually stunning site, **none of it matters if you don't get traffic**.

Websites don't automatically attract leads. If you don't market your site, no one will visit. A common saying from website salespeople and digital marketing companies is, "If you don't have a website, it's like you're invisible online." This saying is true. But what these salespeople and marketing companies don't tell you is this—if you don't market your website, you are **also** invisible online.

Many business owners have this *Field of Dreams* mentality: "If you build it, they will come." But it's just not true. No one is coming unless you market your site. You must actively generate traffic and inbound leads.

Don't get me wrong, a website is important. But it is just the **first step**—not the end result, not the goal.

Marketing is where the real magic happens.

5 proven ways to score inbound leads

In this section, you'll learn about five marketing strategies and actions you can take to get started. This list is not comprehensive. There are dozens of strategies (from email marketing to direct mail, referrals and more). I've chosen to focus on five I've had success with and that I haven't covered enough in other books. With the exception of one sub-tactic, all strategies are focused on inbound leads.

If you're unfamiliar with the term "inbound leads," it refers to prospects who reach out to you, instead of the other way around. More and more, this is where the marketing world is heading, so my aim is to prepare your business for the future.

11.

SEO: The #1 strategy to rank in Google's top 5 search results

No, it's not keywords.

Keywords tend to be what comes to mind when people think of SEO. And while they can be effective, there's a better way to get more bang for your SEO buck:

Backlinks.

What the heck is a backlink? Let me break it down.

A backlink is created when a website links to your content. You've probably seen them before. If you read Entrepreneur or Forbes, you may see articles cite another website using a link. Here's an example from my old blog on ordinarydudemeditation.com:

7. Cuddle your worries away

Grab your sweetheart, hop on the bed or couch and get a little touchy, feely—without the sexy time. No, I'm not talking about cuddle, to foreplay, to sex. I'm talking about cuddle to cuddle, and that's it.

Cuddling has been proven to help ease stress. In fact, there are even businesses in parts of the US that sell cuddling services for just this reason. Basically, you walk into one of these places as if it were a massage parlor (without the happy ending) and cuddle with a complete stranger. It's completely platonic.

The reason cuddling works is because our bodies crave human touch. So the next time you're anxious, don't reach for an oolong tea, reach for your sweetheart and cuddle your worries away.

The blue text links to WebMD. This acts as a backlink that will give WebMD an SEO boost.

Backlinks help search engines determine how high in search results a piece of content should rank. They're like a vote of confidence in your site. I mean, people will only cite good content, right? That's the general philosophy here. When a website backlinks to another, that site inadvertently tells Google, Yahoo, Bing, etc. that the linked page is trustworthy. The search engine then increases the rank of said page, which makes that content easier to find online.

Backlinks are the most powerful way to succeed with SEO fast. But speaking of time, let's define the word "fast" in SEO terms.

How long does it take to gain traction with SEO?

SEO is a long-term marketing strategy. In fact, it's one of the longest, long-term strategies in this book. It can take anywhere from several months to several years to see results.

The reason is pretty simple—search engines don't like one hit wonders or fly-by-night websites. The longer a website exists, the more credibility it has in Google's eyes. What's more, the tactics required to win with SEO take time. You need to develop relationships and create lots of backlink-worthy content.

So if it's such a time suck, why bother?

Because once you rank well, you could save literally millions of dollars in advertising and gain "free" traffic. If you sell a popular product, SEO success basically gives you the right to print money, as all that traffic comes your way on autopilot. Think about it this way: If 5% of all visitors to your website buy a product, then the more visitors to your site, the more money you make. Now imagine that ranking #10 on Google's first page for a certain keyword produces 100 visitors per month. That's five sales. If you can rank in the #3 spot for the same keyword, you might get 5,000 visitors per month and 250 sales—a 50x increase!

In other words, the rewards are lucrative if you persevere.

Adam Enfroy provides a great example of how you can succeed with SEO quickly. He actually gained SEO results faster than anyone I've heard of, going from 0 to 44,000 visitors in six months. Don't get me wrong, the dude worked his ass off, working 100+ hour weeks for months. But his story is well worth reading.

Action items

Now that you have an understanding of SEO and backlinks, here's how to get started:

Write guest posts

As mentioned in *Instant Credibility Online*, guest posting is not dead. In fact, it's a great tactic to win backlinks. As a bonus, guest posting can provide a big credibility boost, especially if you land on Mashable, HuffPost or other popular sites.

That said, developing the writing chops to land guest posts takes time. So I would suggest outsourcing the process to a pro, or enrolling in a course to improve your writing. I highly recommend all Jon Morrow's programs: Serious Bloggers Only, Freedom Machine and Content Marketing Certification. I've tried all of them and they've helped me grow immensely as a writer.

Give testimonials

Giving testimonials can provide you with more than just good feelings for helping someone. You can also get backlinks. How? Just offer your vendors a testimonial in exchange for a backlink. Some will say "no" and still want the testimonial, but it's worth a try.

Offer to be a case study

Similar to testimonials, you can also ask vendors if they'd like to feature your success story in a case study and, again, give you a backlink.

Build relationships

What do all of the above have in common? They require relationship building. Outside these methods, look for opportunities in your normal life to build connections. Perhaps you can get a backlink from your local coffee shop or family doctor. Why not ask them?

Just a quick word of warning: the backlink should make sense. For example, if you own a restaurant or candy shop, a link from a cafe would work, but one from a plumber not so much. Search engines are smart. They can tell if someone tries to game the system by getting links from any

Tom, Dick or Sally. So ensure it makes sense, and shoot for quality over quantity.

12.

Blogging: The secret to blogging success

Blogging. The word probably sounds as exciting as yesterday's underwear.

Let's face it, blogging has been around for a looooooong time. You may have heard stories of a few lucky bloggers who became millionaires and dozens (if not hundreds) who've failed. Perhaps you're one of the latter. No worries. There's nothing to be ashamed of. Blogging is hard, and that's why I want to share shortcuts with you from my near decade of experience as a blogger.

Now, let me be clear. The suggestions I'll make in this chapter aren't meant to make you an online celebrity, like Pat Flynn or Perez Hilton.

Instead, the metric we'll focus on is traffic—in the thousands of visitors per month range. While this may sound like a lot, it's not unreachable. All it takes is a couple handfuls of winning blogs that hook readers and get backlinks. That's right, blogging and SEO overlap significantly.

Blogging, in its essence, is an SEO tactic. One rockstar blog post can gain hundreds of backlinks, bring you monthly inbound leads and raise your search engine rankings.

But not all blogs are created equal. Quality is important when it comes to winning traffic. In my book *Instant Credibility Online*, I go into detail about three different quality levels of blogs. Here's a summary of those below:

- **Low tier: Poorly written blog with generic content** - Defining characteristics of these blogs are generic headlines, typos, awkward sentences and lack of flow.
- **Mid tier: Blog with repurposed, obvious content** - Respun content from other articles, which is not always a bad thing. The advice given is usually pretty obvious, unless you're a beginner.
- **Top tier: Unique, empathic content** - The holy grail of blogging. These blogs use the word "you" often, have a USP and have subheads written like an article headline.

To succeed with blogging, your content must be at least mid-tier, though top-tier can win you traffic quicker. That said, quality is only one part of the story.

What is your audience searching for? 3 ways to find out

For your blog to get traffic, you need to know what your audience is searching for. What questions are on their minds? What are they typing into Google? Which topics capture their attention? The answers will guide your content creation. Let's explore three methods to discover what your audience wants.

1. Use keyword research tools

Let's start with the most obvious, and possibly one you've heard of: keyword research. If you're unfamiliar with this, keyword research enables you to identify how many times Google shows search results for specific search terms. Explaining the keyword research process is beyond the scope of this book and somewhat pointless because each tool works slightly differently. So what I'd like to do here is suggest some tools for you to try:

- Ahrefs - Starting at $99 a month
- Semrush - Starting at $119.95 a month
- KWFinder - Starting at $29.90 a month
- Keysearch - Starting at $17 a month
- Ubersuggest - Free
- Moz Keyword Explorer - Free

Note, this is just the tip of the iceberg. There are dozens of tools out there. If you're just starting out, I'd suggest testing the free or more affordable ones before splurging on something as awesome and advanced as Ahrefs.

2. Know your prospects' questions

All blogs must deliver value to their target audience. One way to do that is to answer their questions. "Easier said than done," you may think. I mean, you can't read your prospects' minds, right? So how can you know their questions? You can ask or survey your subscribers, search internet forums for questions or use a site like Answer The Public: https://answerthepublic.com/

Once you find out your prospects' questions, write posts that answer them in detail.

3. Identify common themes in trending blog posts

If multiple posts about a similar idea go viral, that topic likely resonates with an audience. So in this last suggestion, your job is to identify common themes of recent viral posts in your niche and write your own spin on the topic. Again, you may think, "How the heck do I find common themes?" It's actually pretty easy.

You just need to use a tool like BuzzSumo or Exploding Topics to see which articles are trending, and then analyze the headlines for patterns. Let me show you some examples of how to do this.

Below are four headlines of viral posts I found on BuzzSumo. What do you think the common theme is?

Headlines

- *Why People-Pleasers Don't Get the Love and Respect They Desire* - Tiny Buddha
- *How I Stopped Trying to Please Everyone and Started Prioritizing Myself* - Tiny Buddha
- *How to ditch the guilt of putting yourself first* - Headspace
- *How to stay in bed on Saturday morning and not feel bad about it* - Headspace

I'd say it's something like "Stop people-pleasing, and put yourself first." The article I later wrote on the topic was titled "6 steps to saying 'no' and walking away with a smile."

Let's do one more, just to ensure you get the hang of it...

Headlines

- *Get your mind and body out of crisis mode* - Mindful.org
- *How to boldly move on* - Mindful.org
- *5 Things to Do When You Aren't Hopeful About Anything* - PickTheBrain

- *The Psychology of Momentum: 5 Steps to Get Yourself Out Of A Mental Rut* - PickTheBrain

What's the theme here? "Get out of mental ruts" would be my guess, and the article I later wrote was called "6 steps to igniting hope when your spirits are crushed."

Action items

Now that you know how to find article topics, let's explore a few effective blogging strategies.

Write 1 blog a week

Believe it or not, writing one blog a week does still work, despite what some marketers say. That said, it's not necessarily as efficient as other tactics on this list. The goal here is quantity. If you can write more than one article a week, do it—write as many as possible, answering questions or addressing common concerns in the hope one takes off. It's like baseball. You're not going to hit a home run every time, but if you swing for the fences long enough, you'll knock some out of the park eventually.

Build relationships with bloggers and influencers

Yes, back to the old relationship-building advice. A network of outstanding relationships is like rocket fuel for your business's growth engine. Start by identifying 20 or so influencers and interact with them on a weekly basis, always providing value (whether that's an insightful comment, an article share or review of their latest book). Once you've built relationships, ask the influencers to share your posts. This can generate a big spike of traffic and also get the SEO engines firing if you get backlinks in the process.

Blog for backlinks

As mentioned in the last chapter, backlinks are the number one way to succeed with SEO. In fact, Adam Enfroy recommends not blogging until you've acquired tons of backlinks via guest posts. The reason? Backlinks will get you boatloads of traffic and could save you months, or possibly years, of time from blogging on your own site with few people reading.

All the above tactics can work for your business—the key is consistency. If you give up after a month, three months or even a year, you'll lose traction. If you're going to blog, commit to it. Yes, it's possible to see results in just a month or two, but be prepared for a long road. Because results in blogging aren't guaranteed. You just have to keep trying and testing, which is something we'll discuss at the end of this section.

13.

A book: How becoming an author can grow your business

Writing a book probably sounds like a daunting task to most business owners. I mean, it could take years, right?

Let me tell you this.

I published three books in 2019. Seriously. Now, that doesn't mean I wrote them that year (all were started in 2018). That said, I can complete a book in a three to six month period. And I consider myself slow. I have author buddies who publish at a significantly higher clip than me, some pumping out 10 books a year.

Now, I'm not suggesting you write garbage. I care about quality, and if you read any of my books you'll hopefully see that. But my point is, publishing a book is a realistic option for you—and the benefits can be huge.

The business benefits of publishing a book

Book sales are great. I get a nice passive income of around $1,500 a month in book royalties, and that number is on the rise. That said, for businesses, a book offers much more marketing value for your dollar than just royalties. A teacher of mine, Chandler Bolt, used his book as the growth engine for his now multimillion dollar company. And there are many like him.

A book, when combined with a lead magnet, can generate hundreds of leads a month. For those unfamiliar with lead magnets, they're basically valuable content (like a resource list, cheat sheet, ebook, template, etc.) you offer for free in exchange for a person's email address. Here are two lead magnets I've used:

The above is for my meditation site, ordinarydudemeditation.com.

This one I formerly used for my marketing site, johnweiler.co.

How do you combine a lead magnet with your book?

Simple. Most of the time, you offer the lead magnet in your book's first pages. Here's what it looks like in practice:

Free Gift

From the Dalai Lama to Adyashanti, meditation has served as a critical practice for many enlightened teachers. The below gift makes a perfect partner guide to *An Ordinary Dude's Guide to Enlightenment* as you'll be able to put into practice one of the book's key teachings.

In the **Meditation Starter Guide: What You Need (And What You Don't) To Meditate Today**, you'll learn:

- **Simple instructions** - to meditate in the next 20 minutes
- **How to take your practice anywhere** - learn 3 things needed for each meditation session
- **Money-saving tips** - a list of common paid items you can skip as a new meditator
- **How long it takes to get results** - the number of consistent days of meditation needed to gain more peace, calm and happiness
- **And more...**

Get The Meditation Starter Guide

This guide is a result of my 17+ year meditation practice. And as a thank you for purchasing *An Ordinary Dude's Guide to Enlightenment*, I'd like to give you the Meditation Starter Guide absolutely **free of charge.**

A consistent meditation practice can provide further clarity, peace and happiness on the path to enlightenment. And now you can learn how to do it for free.

Click the link below to get your copy:

I want my Meditation Starter Guide

This lead magnet appears on the fourth page of *An Ordinary Dude's Guide to Enlightenment*. Why does location matter? Because when you publish on platforms like Amazon, Kobo and other retailers, readers can sample your book's beginning for free. If your lead magnet is there, they can download it without purchasing the actual book. But wait. Then you could miss out on book sales, right?

Yes. But for the majority of businesses, a subscriber is worth much more than a book sale. You can sell subscribers on high ticket products or services, which can translate into tens, or even hundreds, of thousands of dollars—far more than a few bucks book royalty.

Credibility is the second major reason to publish a book. Books have a somewhat magical luster as most people aren't authors. A book makes you stand out. It proves you have some authority on a topic. You couldn't possibly write an entire book on a subject if you were clueless, right? Well, that's at least the mindset many people have about authors.

Credibility, however, is not a given. For that, you'll need a professional cover and reviews. A poorly designed cover makes your book look self-published, which could actually hurt your credibility. As for reviews, 10 is good enough to start, but aim for as many as possible because the more reviews you have the more credible you'll appear.

Action items

Now that you understand why a book is a great marketing tool, let's look at how you can succeed:

Write a short book, less than 15,000 words

A book doesn't have to be super long. My shortest one, around 8,000 words, was my best seller for ages, selling around 25 paperback copies a week. The book sold well because it has a brilliant cover, is incredibly unique and ranked high for some lucrative keywords: three important factors for book traffic and sales.

Information is valuable, which is why a short book can work. People don't care about length when they want to solve an excruciatingly painful problem. So consider doing just that for your short book.

Which problem should you cover?

Think about your best selling product or service, and ask yourself, "Which is the most stressful problem it solves?" Write about that and aim for a length of 8,000-15,000 words. Focus on providing value, and readers will begin to trust you.

Repurpose blogs to save time

You can save oodles of time by repurposing your blogs into a book. Now, most people will think of repurposing **published** blogs. While you can use them, there's an easier way.

Instead, I recommend outlining the book first and then writing your individual blog posts based on specific chapters. I've written books this way for myself and clients and, in fact, this book series was written in a similar fashion.

The chapters in ICO and others in the Digital Marketing Success series (including this book you're reading now) are not long. This is intentional. That's because during the outlining process I thought of how I could use chapters as blogs. "Think like a designer," "How many pages? What pages?" and other chapters were originally published as articles on LinkedIn. Is the content in the blog and book exactly the same? It's similar, but no.

Finished book content and blog content look different. My blogs typically include emphatic opens and closes, my books do not. Also, book chapters must flow together, which doesn't always work when you copy and paste blogs into a book. Point being, if you go this route, tweak your content accordingly.

Advertise your book on these 3 platforms

As a new author, you'll likely need to advertise your book to gain leads. The three best platforms for this are Amazon Ads, BookBub and Facebook. Here you can pay less than a dollar (sometimes just 10¢!) per click, which is pretty good, considering a lead could cost you as little as a few bucks.

Out of the three platforms mentioned, I recommend starting with Amazon because it has the smallest learning curve and you're least likely to lose your shirt. Facebook and BookBub can easily blow through your ad budget in a day, whereas Amazon rarely does that (unless it's the holidays or you're bidding in the dollar plus range).

14

Advertising: The most important principle to win sales

Advertising is a broad topic. There are Amazon Ads, Facebook Ads, Google Ads and others, with each platform working differently. If you're new to advertising, you may feel overwhelmed about where to begin or if you should even bother. I won't lie, advertising can be difficult. But there's also a major upside.

Why consider advertising

Advertising is a smart investment because it's a viable short-term marketing strategy. It provides immediate gratification. If you know what you're doing, you can gain instant traffic, sales and leads. That's not to say there isn't risk. If you're a newbie, you can lose lots of money, sometimes very quickly. That's less likely to happen if you're advertising a book on Amazon, but Facebook and Google are a different story.

Facebook has a reputation of ripping through ad dollars. Whatever budget you set each day will likely get spent. As for Google Ads, they are super expensive. While the average cost per click is just a buck or two, some industries charge upwards of $50 for a single click. That does not, however, mean you shouldn't bother with Google. If you have a big advertising budget and are selling high ticket items or services, Google Ads can be a great choice. But I'd recommend hiring an expert for the sake of your own budget.

None of the other marketing methods mentioned in previous chapters can show results in a matter of hours since they're all long-term strategies.

The main problem with advertising

Advertising is the murkiest marketing strategy in this book. While I know some advertisers who earned $10,000+ in profit by the end of their second month, I also know others who've struggled with little to no results for years on end. The strategies that work for selling one product may differ for another and can change from niche to niche. For example, marketing copy that works on sneaker collectors likely won't be effective for those interested in running shoes.

In other words, it's really difficult to give any solid advice about advertising because what works for one person may not work for the next. But there is one piece of advice I can offer. In my half decade experience in ads and hundreds of conversations I've had with fellow advertisers, there is a common theme. Something that everyone who's found some level of success can agree on.

The most important principle in advertising

No, it's not the copywriting, ad imagery, number of ads run or the size of your budget. The principle is far simpler. In fact, it's so simple many new advertisers overlook it completely. So what is it?

Targeting. If you don't get your targeting right, you're destined for failure. Oddly enough, this comes back to a common theme in this book: you need to know your audience. Who are they? What are their interests? How old are they? Answering these questions will help you find customers.

Does that mean your ad copy and design don't matter? No, they must also be good, but again, what is "good" depends on your audience.

For example, take the 2006 McDonald's Hummer Happy Meal flop. The global fast food giant partnered with the truck brand to create a toy line. It didn't go well. Parents and environmentalist groups fumed, especially when both companies admitted the campaign was really aimed at parents, hoping it would encourage them to buy Hummers.

Now, think about this from a targeting perspective. Is the average McDonald's eater someone who would buy a Hummer? Probably not. Hummers are extremely expensive cars, and McDonald's, well, they have the dollar menu. Now, that doesn't mean Hummer owners never eat McDonald's, I'm sure some do. The point is, the campaign was marketing a niche product to a massive and diverse audience. They were using a wide net, instead of a spear gun.

Keep this story in mind as you begin your advertising journey. All the ad platforms offer granular targeting options. And the more finely refined your audience is, the more precisely your spear gun fires, the more likely you'll succeed.

Action items

Besides highly targeted ads, I have only one recommended action item for new advertisers:

Choose one platform to start

Yes, it's that simple. If you forego outsourcing and advertise yourself, start with a single platform. Learning advertising is an art in itself. It takes time to master design, copywriting and other skills, and you'll likely fail considerably along the way.

Since there's a steep learning curve, you should only advertise with money you're willing to lose. Because there's a good chance you'll lose all of it in the beginning. Think of these financial losses as an investment: learn from them and you'll gain invaluable experience.

Only explore other ad platforms once you start regularly gaining a profit. As for which platform to begin with, if you have a book with a lead magnet inside, I can't recommend Amazon enough. Facebook is a solid starting place for other businesses.

15.

Social Media: 3 strategies to reel in leads

Social media is a hot button topic. Many business owners say it doesn't work—don't believe them.

Over the past three years, social media has been my number one source of new business. Most business owners fail because they're doing it wrong. They're thinking about it the wrong way, posting without purpose or strategic planning.

In this chapter, I'll show you proven strategies that have worked for myself and my clients.

3 ways to win with social media

1. Join groups

You've probably seen groups on Facebook and LinkedIn. To succeed in them, you first need to establish yourself as an expert within the group: post helpful content, answer questions and show up regularly to win members' trust.

This won't happen overnight. But once you've consistently offered value and become a familiar face, which will likely take a few months, that's when the magic happens.

You start getting referrals and inquiries. Of course, for this to occur, you need to be vocal about your services. No, this doesn't mean you SPAM the group, constantly selling them. But you should make an effort to answer questions specifically about your services and, every once in a while, subtly mention them.

Also, be ready to pounce when a member posts they're looking for a service provider. This is not the time to be shy. Respond to the post, tell them what you offer, share your USP and ask to connect with them privately.

Again, this is all about being strategic. I've won several new clients following this method, and it can work for you as well.

2. Build relationships with influencers

Befriend an influencer, and you may suddenly win access to tens of thousands of their followers. Here's one approach I recommend.

Follow the same steps I outlined for joining groups: join the influencer's community, and position yourself as a helpful member and expert. Be sure to also interact with the influencer when he/she posts. Don't force it. But when it seems natural, respond to the influencer's post or add a thoughtful comment.

I should note, you don't necessarily have to join an influencer's group (he/she may not have one). Instead you can connect with them online and follow the same process: leave helpful comments, answer other followers' questions and, basically, offer value. If you'd like to learn more about this process, check out the "Endorsements" chapter in *Instant Credibility Online.*

The second way to build influencer relationships is through blogging. One way to do this is by writing a roundup post, which is when you curate great content within a niche or on a specific topic. Some sample headlines could be: "15 creative ways to lose 10 lbs in 2 weeks" and "21 expert graphic design predictions for 2022." Whoever your target influencers are, name them and link to their content in the post.

Another method is to name the best influencers in your niche. You could use a blog headline like "The 37 smartest SEO gurus online" or "The 9 green revolution leaders in household cleaning products." Whatever your industry is, just name it in the headline as well as a flattering name for the influencers: "SEO gurus," "Green revolution leaders," etc.

If you use the roundup or "best influencer" style post, be sure to tell the influencers you mentioned them, either through email, social media or other means. If they don't know about your post, then you won't build the relationships.

Last but not least, don't forget the advice in Chapter 12 about asking influencers to share your posts. This can be another way to win influencer traffic.

3. LOIs

The marketing section of this book is focused on inbound leads. But I'd like to share one non-inbound strategy. Why? Because I've used it to score several dream clients. LOI stands for Letter Of Introduction, and it's basically a cold email to prospects—like the email version of a cold call.

If you've done LOIs before and failed, you probably need to change your strategy. The key is to send your LOI to the right person at the right company. This requires research. In fact, you'll spend 50% or more of your time researching companies than sending LOIs.

Similar to the Advertising Chapter, the key to success is targeting. If you find the right target, in terms of niche and size of company (bigger companies pay more), you could land a dream client, too.

Who should you contact in the companies you want to work with? It will vary from industry to industry, but basically decision makers. For me as a writer, it's Marketing Directors, as they typically choose a company's service providers. If you're selling a product, it could be the CEO, VP of Sales, Product Lead, etc.

How do you research? You can use Google, the Fortune 500 or 1,000 lists, lists of fastest growing companies, the Crunchbase Daily newsletter, etc. That said, I highly recommend LinkedIn, specifically their Sales Navigator or higher membership plans. You can do quite a bit of research on the free version, but it will take at least twice as long. Most business owners and freelancers who actively use LinkedIn to find leads can save enough time and find enough data to make LinkedIn's paid plans worth the cost.

Pro tip: Never send emails to addresses without names. For example, info@marketingmavericks.com, contact@bakerybuddies.com. Your message may get directed to the wrong person, buried underneath hundreds of other random messages or deleted for no good reason. If you use LI Sales Navigator, you can contact decision makers directly using InMails. Alternatively, I use the two services below to find email addresses of the exact people I want to contact:

- https://hunter.io/
- https://www.voilanorbert.com/

Action items

What I'm about to tell you isn't rocket science. In fact, it's quite obvious. But the majority of people won't follow through and will write off social media, saying it doesn't work. When really it was their process that caused them to fail. So here's what you need to do:

Show up

Whatever strategy you choose, whether groups, influencer outreach or even LOIs, **be consistent**. You won't gain traction otherwise. The group members will forget about you as will the influencers. And as for LOIs, they can take months of trial and error before you see success.

So be active in groups or interact with your target influencers two or three times a week. Send 20-30 LOIs a week. Now this doesn't mean you have to do all three strategies mentioned in this chapter. Just choose one to start. Get going with that, show up week after week and you will eventually see results in the coming months.

Your Edge—Marketing

Successful marketing usually comes down to principles—there isn't one magic strategy that works for everyone. So think of marketing like an experiment. Which brings us to our first of three tactical advantages.

The Pick 2 Focus

We live in a world where it's hard to focus. We're distracted by the latest advertisement, email notification or phone call. There are so many possible paths we can take, so many options that we freeze up. Stuck in decision paralysis. We do nothing. So my advice to you is, choose only two marketing strategies to start. More than that and you risk spreading your attention thin, which could ultimately destroy your productivity, results and morale. Trust me. I'm speaking from experience.

So peel through the marketing strategies in this section, and choose the two most appealing. Ideally, you want to select one short and one long-term strategy:

- SEO: Long-term
- Blogging: Long-term
- Book: Long-term
- Ads: Short-term

- Social Media: Short-term

What happens if your chosen strategies become a bust or a drag? Switch.

Think of yourself as a marketing scientist, experimenting with different compounds (strategies) until you find a combination that is both effective and enjoyable. Try your strategies for three to six months, analyze your results and enthusiasm for them, then decide to stay the course or try something else. Rinse and repeat.

Bear in mind, some strategies can take much longer than six months to prove effective. That's where this next principle comes in.

Test, pivot, test

Just because your two strategies don't work after six months, doesn't necessarily mean you should switch tactics. SEO is a great example. It could take years to see results. So if you're enjoying SEO, but not making progress after six months, maybe your SEO strategy is the problem. You could be targeting the wrong keywords, or you could have low quality backlinks.

The point is, you may need to try different sub-strategies within your core strategy.

If your book sales suck after six months, what could be wrong? The issue may be a poor cover, lack of reviews or a weak title. So try changing one of these things. You won't know what's wrong unless you test.

Every single strategy in this guide requires testing along the way. You must make minor pivots until you find what works. I do this myself.

For example, my first book launch failed miserably. It took me over a year to identify the problem, and then suddenly I went from selling a few books a month to 100+. What had I been doing wrong? I was selling books on my own new website, which lacked credibility, and I wasn't advertising. Once I corrected those two issues, sales multiplied 10x.

Had I never tested ads or tried selling on Amazon, the book you're reading right now wouldn't exist. It was only because that first book began to do well that I wrote another, and another, and now I have 13 published.

I hope you're starting to see why testing and making small pivots is crucial. If you don't, you'll remain stuck—no matter how good your copywriting or design is. So read books, take courses, get mentors. Learn from their mistakes to gain faster results. Test, test and test again. It's critical to your marketing success.

Diversify your marketing

Once you find one successful marketing strategy, don't stop. If you regularly read business books, you've probably heard authors tout the benefits of focusing on one thing. As you can probably tell, I too somewhat encourage "less is more" thinking with my Pick 2 Focus principle. But by less, I don't mean one thing. I just mean don't focus on a dozen things, or even a half dozen.

Diversification is important because a marketing strategy that works today might not tomorrow. And if all your eggs are in one basket, it could destroy your business if that marketing strategy ever dries up.

For example, if you rely solely on SEO, what would happen if Google were to make a drastic algorithm change that knocked you down to the bottom of search results?

You'd be screwed. You could go from selling hundreds of products a week to zero. But if you had also been successfully advertising on Facebook, then you'd probably be okay. Sure, the SEO hit would hurt, but the Facebook sales should tide you over till you pivot or find a new strategy altogether.

Diversification is key in marketing. Once you find something that works, find another and then another. Somewhere between two and four strategies should be enough to ensure continual business growth no matter what happens to the economy or the platforms you leverage.

Conclusion

The future of online business

"There is so much stuff that has yet to be invented. There's so much new that's going to happen. People don't have any idea yet how impactful the internet is going to be and that this is still Day 1 in such a big way." - Jeff Bezos

Congratulations, you've reached the end of this book. By now, you have a solid foundation of digital knowhow to reinvent your business online.

But wait.

What if the practices in this book change? What if by the time you implement them, they no longer work?

I have some good news.

Marketing strategies may evolve and gurus may write new books about copywriting and design, but the basics you've learned here are timeless.

For example, yesterday's brochure is now a website, sales letters have evolved into landing pages and the once popular newspaper ad has become a Facebook ad. The marketing methods of yesterday are still around, they've just taken new forms.

What's more, the copywriting and design principles you learned aren't concepts I invented. The USP was coined in the 1960s by advertising exec Rosser Reeves and the "simple design" tip I suggest in the "Your Edge" section of Part 1 has been prevalent in marketing for over a hundred years, as evident by the old Shell Oil (1904) and Bass Ale (1876) logos.

If you've read *The Website Homepage Blueprint*, you also know that emotion has been used to persuade since Aristotle's days. And I wouldn't be surprised if many of this book's tactics were applied 5,000+ years ago in ancient Egypt. Maybe a gold or ivory shop seller created a classy, luxurious buying environment for his high class clientele, all while selling the dream of how his products make them the center of attention at parties and feasts.

Where will your business be in 5 years?

Will you have reinvented it online? Or will you have stayed the same, praying the customer still walks through your brick and mortar doors?

As ecommerce sends malls and main streets the way of the dinosaur, you have a once-in-a-lifetime opportunity to get into the game now, ahead of so many others. And if you have a proven product or service, chances are it will sell just as well online.

Start your online transition today and you could double, triple or even quadruple your profits within five years. How would that change your life? Would it free up your schedule to spend quality time with your family? Would it earn you enough to buy your dream home? Would it provide you more money to invest in your business, grow it faster and make a larger impact on the world and your community?

Reinventing your business online can open the door to many opportunities and a new life. I don't want to pretend that this road is easy or fast. It's not. Following through with the tactics outlined in this book will take time, focus and perseverance.

But you **can** do it if you take this process one step at a time.

So commit to yourself today that you will reinvent your business online.

Focus on a few strategies first, build on them and soon enough your efforts will snowball.

Also by John Weiler

The bestselling *Digital Marketing Success* series

Endnotes

Introduction

2 According to leading ecommerce research company. April Berthene, "Coronavirus pandemic adds $219 billion to US ecommerce sales in 2020-2021," Digital Commerce 360, Mar 15, 2022. https://www.digitalcommerce360.com/article/coronavirus-impact-online-retail/

4 According to Ahrefs. Tim Soulo, "90.63% of Content Gets No Traffic From Google. And How to Be in the Other 9.37% [New Research for 2020]," ahrefs blog, January 31, 2020. https://ahrefs.com/blog/search-traffic-study/

Chapter 1

16 Check out SEO guru. Neil Patel, Neil Patel, accessed September 18, 2022. https://neilpatel.com/

19 Jon Morrow's excellent. Jon Morrow, Smart Blogger, accessed September 18, 2022. https://smartblogger.com/

Chapter 2

22 In Joe Sugarman's book. Joseph Sugarman, *The Adweek Copywriting Handbook: The Ultimate Guide to Writing Powerful Advertising and Marketing Copy from One of America's Top Copywriters* (New Jersey: John Wiley & Sons, Inc., 2007), chap. 6, Kindle.

Chapter 3

35 Like IBM. IBM, accessed September 18, 2022. https://www.ibm.com/us-en/

35 Or Apple. Apple, accessed September 18, 2022. https://www.apple.com/

35 By Chris Guillebeau. Chris Guillebeau, The Art of Non-Conformity, accessed September 18, 2022. https://chrisguillebeau.com/

35 Or ClickFunnels. Russell Brunson, ClickFunnels, accessed September 18, 2022. https://www.clickfunnels.com/

36 According to HubSpot. Anna Fitzgerald, "What Is the Average Time Spent On a Website? [+ How to Improve It]," HubSpot, December 22, 2021. https://blog.hubspot.com/marketing/chartbeat-website-engagement-data-nj#sm.00000jze5p9jn4esluajqn5p1bqxi

37 Creating a one-page. Adam Heitzman, "Single-Page Websites: Are They Good Or Bad For SEO?," Search Engine Journal, April 18, 2022. https://www.searchenginejournal.com/single-page-websites-good-bad-seo/190095/#close

Your Edge—Design

57 Simplicity is a deliberate design strategy. Chip Heath and Dan Heath, *Made to Stick: Why Some Ideas Survive and Others Die* (New York: Random House, 2007), chap. 1, Kindle.

58 The theme of *It*. *It: Special Edition*, directed by Andrés Muschietti (2018; Warner Brothers), DVD.

58 The *Arrival* theme. *Arrival*, directed by Denis Villeneuve (2017; Paramount), DVD.

Chapter 6

62 Research has shown activates. Dennis P. Carmody and Michael Lewis, "Brain Activation When Hearing One's Own and Others' Names," National Center for Biotechnology Information, September 7, 2006. https://www.ncbi.nlm.nih.gov/pmc/articles/PMC1647299/

62 According to famous marketer. Neil Patel, Neil Patel, "Use These 3 Power Words To Boost Conversion Rates," Neil Patel, accessed September 10, 2022. https://neilpatel.com/blog/boost-conversion-rate/

Chapter 7

66 In the movie *Elf*. *Elf*, directed by Jon Favreau (2008; Warner Brothers), Blu-ray.

69 Jeff Bezos was enamored with Sam Walton. Brad Stone, *The Everything Store: Jeff Bezos And The Age of Amazon* (New York: Back Bay Books, 2013).

70 A concept developed by the car manufacturer. Kathy Van der Herten, "Did you know ...who invented the five whys principle?," LinkedIn Pulse, August 21, 2020. https://www.linkedin.com/pulse/did-you-know-who-invented-five-whys-principle-kathy-van-der-herten/. There seems to be a debate about who invented the 5 Whys. Most sources say it's Sakichi Toyoda while a few claim it as Taiichi Ohno. I ultimately settled on Taiichi as the Sakichi sources mentioned the technique was developed in the 1930s and Sakichi died in the year 1930. As it seems somewhat doubtful Sakichi would develop such a revolutionary technique in the last year of his life, the referenced link claims Taiichi developed it. If you can prove the true source, feel free to email me about it and I'll update this citation accordingly.

Chapter 9

79 According to MarketingProfs. Puranjay Singh, "2 Million Blog Posts Are Written Every Day, Here's How You Can Stand Out," MarketingProfs, accessed September 10, 2022. https://www.marketingprofs.com/articles/2015/27698/2-million-blog-posts-are-written-every-day-heres-how-you-can-stand-out

Chapter 10

92 Tough guys doing tough things. Donald Miller, *Building a StoryBrand* course, MentorBox, MentorBox video. https://www.mentorbox.com/course/building-a-story-brand. The story cited is within one of the individual lessons in Donald Miller's *Building a StoryBrand* MentorBox course. MentorBox is a paid subscription service. As I'm no longer a member, I can't recall which lesson the Aspirational Identity is discussed. If you're reading this and know, feel free to contact me and I'll update this citation accordingly.

Your Edge—Copywriting

96 Jon Morrow offers. Jon Morrow, "801+ Power Words That Pack a Punch & Convert like Crazy," Smart Blogger, Aug 25, 2022. https://smartblogger.com/power-words/

Chapter 11

105 Adam Enfroy provides a great example. Adam Enfroy, "My Story: Battling Self Doubt to Blogging Success," Adam Enfroy, accessed September 10, 2022. https://www.adamenfroy.com/my-story

Chapter 12

114 In fact, Adam Enfroy recommends. Adam Enfroy, "How to Make Money Blogging in 2022 ($200k Per Month)," Adam Enfroy, July 7, 2022. https://www.adamenfroy.com/how-to-make-money-blogging. At one point, I believe Enfroy specifically said not to regularly blog until you've acquired tons of backlinks. While I can no longer find that statement, he gives that impression on this page and throughout his site.

Chapter 14

126 Take the 2006 McDonald's. "Spectacular advertising flops and why they failed," accessed July 20, 2021. https://www.thebalancecareers.com/spactacular-advertising-flops-and-why-they-failed-39177. This article is where I obtained the original details of the story, but it looks like it's no longer accessible. If you'd like to learn more about the details of this ad campaign, just Google "2006 McDonald's hummer happy meal ad campaign" and you're likely to find lots of articles on the topic.

Conclusion

140 There is so much stuff. Brad Stone, *The Everything Store: Jeff Bezos And The Age of Amazon* (New York: Back Bay Books, 2013).

141 The USP was coined. Matt Duxbury, "The unique selling proposition: A brief history," Upp, May 15, 2017. https://www.uppb2b.co.uk/insights/branding/unique-selling-proposition-brief-history/

141 The "simple design" tip. Thomas C. Frohlich and Alexander Kent, "Ten Oldest Company Logos in the World," 24/7 Wall St., June 19, 2014. https://247wallst.com/special-report/2014/06/19/10-oldest-company-logos-in-the-world/2/

Made in United States
Orlando, FL
04 November 2026

90218654R00088